CAMPUS gODS

CAMPUS gODS

Exposing the idols that can
derail your present
and destroy your future

GUY CHMIELESKI

Copyright 2013 by Guy Chmieleski

All rights reserved. No part of this publication may be reproduced, stored in a retrieval system, or transmitted, in any form or by any means—electronic, mechanical, photocopying, recording, or otherwise—without prior written permission, except for brief quotations in critical reviews or articles.

All Scripture quotations, unless otherwise noted, are taken from THE HOLY BIBLE, NEW INTERNATIONAL VERSION®, NIV® Copyright © 1973, 1978, 1984, 2011 by Biblica, Inc.™ Used by permission. All rights reserved worldwide.

Scripture quotations marked ESV are taken from the Holy Bible: English Standard Version, copyright © 2001, Wheaton: Good News Publishers. Used by permission. All rights reserved.

Scripture quotations marked NLT are taken from the Holy Bible, New Living Translation, copyright 1996, 2004. Used by permission of Tyndale House Publishers, Inc., Wheaton, Illinois 60189. All rights reserved.

Scripture quotations marked THE MESSAGE are taken from *The Message* Copyright © by Eugene H. Peterson 1993, 1994, 1995, 1996, 2000, 2001, 2002. Used by permission of NavPress Publishing Group.

Printed in the United States of America

Paperback ISBN: 978-1-62824-050-4
Mobi ISBN: 978-1-62824-051-1
ePub ISBN: 978-1-62824-052-8
uPDF ISBN: 978-1-62824-053-5

Library of Congress Control Number: 2013950432

Cover design by Andrew Dragos
Page design by PerfecType, Nashville, TN

SEEDBED PUBLISHING
Sowing for a Great Awakening
204 N. Lexington Avenue, Wilmore, Kentucky 40390
www.seedbed.com

*To my sweet wife Heather and our five energetic kids.
You make my life full and fun!*

*To the students who bring shape to my days and my work.
You encourage and challenge me.*

*To the God who has blessed me with love and life.
You give me the strength and direction to fulfill the roles
and opportunities You bring my way.*

I am the light of the world.
Whoever follows me will never walk in darkness,
but will have the light of life.
(Jesus *in John 8:12*)

CONTENTS

FOREWORD / xi

FIRST WORDS >> The Hole in Our Souls / 1

Exposing the CAMPUS gODS

god of ACHIEVEMENT / 17

god of FREEDOM / 31

god of STATUS / 45

god of SUBSTANCES / 61

god of PLEASURE / 77

god of INTIMACY / 93

god of INFORMATION / 107

god of VOICE / 121

god of (IR)RESPONSIBILITY / 133

god of NEW / 149

LAST WORDS >> A New Creation / 161

NOTES / 165

FOREWORD

Every August campus ministers prepare for the flood of young adults who will venture through academic buildings and residence halls with their backpacks, iPads, laptops, and earbuds, looking to connect into WiFi and filter through the barrage of opportunities available to them. From academic challenges to athletic scholarships to social clubs to leadership positions, the competition for their time and attention is intense. As students navigate where they will focus externally, they also must decide where their internal passion will be drawn. What are their motivations? Who and what will their hearts bow toward?

For over twenty years, I have served Jesus in the university world. We campus ministers minister to a virtual parade of students, who pass by us as we metaphorically hand out cups of cold water on the parade route, in the name of Jesus. We offer friendship, pastoral direction, and care, and get the raw and beautiful gift of seeing God woo the hearts of young adults.

Often that wooing happens through the messy reality of life. It happens when, again and again, we see students trip and fall and find themselves aware of their desperate need of a Savior. As the

Gungor song says, God makes "beautiful things out of the dust" and "beautiful things out of us." God works with us in the midst of the broken pieces of life. God is certainly doing that work among university students—restoring and preparing them for a life lived abundantly with service and love.

However, it's clear that there is competition for the minds, bodies and souls of these young adults. I see the pulls of status, achievement, information overload, pleasure without boundaries, consumer-style intimacy, and a constant drive for "the new" waging war against God's invitation to the full, abundant Life. If you are a young adult, you know the intensity of the pressure to live life at the foot of the "campus gods." Although the pull toward these gods has always been present, today's snare of 24/7 technology and social inundation keeps students more easily within their grasp. The gods around you are demanding and unrelenting in their pursuit of not only your present, but your future. This book can be your guide to discerning the traps that lay open and ready for you in these hugely pivotal years of young adulthood.

Dr. Guy Chmieleski—an expert student-ologist who leads the national conversation on campus ministry as a blogger, presenter, author, conference convener, and practitioner—speaks to the heart of the matter from the real life stories of university students in the midst of working out what it means to follow Jesus. Without pat answers or platitudes, he exposes the false idols that most often capture the hearts of students. Not only does Guy identify the traps, but he also provides practical tools to reorient oneself around God's heart and invitation. He speaks not from behind a pulpit or from a church office, but from the settings of daily ministry with college students: coffee shops, retreats, spring break trips, and classrooms.

As I turned the pages of this book, I found myself thinking of students I wanted to share it with, and I also realized that it speaks to me directly. I am grateful for Guy putting into words what he has hashed out, practiced, and lived into through the years in his relationships with students.

I will give this book to my student leaders and to my colleagues and friends who minister to students. If you are a student, or just someone who cares about them, *CAMPUS gODS* will challenge you and expose the idols that can trip all of us up. I pray that as you read it, your heart and mind will be open to the work of the Holy Spirit in your life. If you are like me, I think you will find that it speaks to your story and the stories of the young adults you know. The Holy Spirit offers Life and hope, and gives grace, redemption, and restoration. The Spirit calls you—and all of us—to be people of God who live life at the feet of Jesus.

Dr. Sarah Thomas Baldwin
University Pastor and Dean of Spiritual Life
George Fox University
August 2013

FIRST WORDS >>

THE HOLE IN OUR SOULS

Dear children, keep yourselves from idols.
1 John 5:21

I love the band Mumford & Sons! Their songs are filled with incredibly rich language, and one of their songs, "Roll Away Your Stone" (from their debut studio album *Sigh No More*), includes a vivid and poetic expression of the reality of the human condition. The song writers use words like darkness, hole, soul, substance, void, and character as they attempt to describe and comprehend what they see in the world.

It's clear that they believe life involves the search for something, and yet so much of what they see seems bleak. They can't believe it's really as bad as it appears, and yet the prevalence and pervasive nature of the darkness is overwhelming.

The song seems to spotlight a big part of the crisis I'm seeing on so many of today's college campuses: young souls with growing, gaping holes—and futile attempts to fill those holes with sundry different things, many of which are incredibly harmful.

I agree with Mumford & Sons; darkness is a harsh term, indeed. As I look about today's campus, I see too many students stumbling around in the darkness, trying to find their way, with little success to show for their efforts.

>>

I've been a pastor to college students since 1997, and I wanted to write regarding the major crisis happening all around you. Maybe it's even happening within you.

This struggle is often much easier to see in others than it is in yourself. And trust me when I say that no one is immune to the potential perils that lie in wait all over campus.

How do I know?

Because I've had a front-row seat since I graduated from college and started working with college students.

You see, there's a battle taking place for your soul.

There's an Enemy who is cunning and deceptive. The Bible makes reference to a number of names he might be known by, but he's universally known as the Devil or Satan. And this Enemy knows how to expose your weaknesses, prey on your insecurities, and take advantage of your missteps.

What I see on campus

Many of today's college students arrive on campus and rather quickly begin to sense confusion about who they are—and *whose* they are. And to a degree, this makes sense. College is a time of major life transition.

But too many students seem to struggle to understand how the faith that shaped their growing-up years—the one that they brought with them to campus—now fits into their new college context. They cannot see its relevance. And they're unable to see how it's meant to shape their relationships, education, priorities, and purpose in life during these incredibly formative years.

And for a season, they'll think they're doing OK. Everyone does—until it's too late.

Can you relate? Does any of this sound familiar to you?

If you're like many of the students I've encountered, you have moments of being acutely aware of just how deep your struggles are. But instead of reaching out for help, you'll be tempted to mask it from the rest of the world. "I'm fine," you'll say to those who might ask, and you'll try to convince yourself that those words are even partially true. But deep down you'll know better.

Instead of turning to God and asking for help with issues at the core of your identity, you may attempt to manage the feelings of insecurity, pain, or confusion you're experiencing. You may choose to deal with your struggles by vigorously pursuing a variety of other things that may provide moments of relief, but nothing that is long-lasting.

Maybe you'll follow the lead of your friends, even though most of them are just as confused, desperate, broken, and fearful as you.

Maybe you'll consider asking someone older and wiser for help, but it will likely be a fleeting thought, because somewhere inside you have come to believe that you're supposed to have it all figured out by now. You won't want to appear weak, muddled, or out of control. But that pride will further complicate your struggles.

Remember, the Enemy is here to expose your weaknesses, prey on your insecurities, and take advantage of your missteps.

And in an attempt to deal with your struggles, you'll probably find yourself pursuing things that might make you feel good, comfortable, successful, or complete, believing that they will fill that hole deep inside your soul. Academics, relationships, partying, pleasure, new toys—they're all possible places you might focus your attention and energies, believing that it will cure what ails you.

But no matter how hard you try, finding your identity in anything (or anyone) other than God will yield you minimal and, ultimately, short-lived results.

I hope this book will serve you in ways similar to the apostle Paul's plea to the Greeks in Athens when he proclaimed:

> *It is plain to see that you Athenians take your religion seriously. When I arrived here the other day, I was fascinated with all the shrines I came across. And then I found one inscribed,* TO THE GOD NOBODY KNOWS. *I'm here to introduce you to this God so you can worship intelligently, know who you're dealing with.*

> *The God who made the world and everything in it, this Master of sky and land, doesn't live in custom-made shrines or need the human race to run errands for him, as if he couldn't take care of himself. He makes the creatures; the creatures don't make him. Starting from scratch, he made the entire human race and made the earth hospitable, with plenty of time and space for living so we could seek after God, and not just grope around in the dark but actually* find *him. He doesn't play hide-and-seek with us. He's not remote; he's near. We live and move in him, can't get away from him! One of your poets said it well: "We're the God-created." Well, if we are the God-created, it doesn't make a lot of sense to think we could hire a sculptor to chisel a god out of stone for us, does it?*

God overlooks it as long as you don't know any better—but that time is past. The unknown is now known, and he's calling for a radical life-change. (Acts 17:22–30 The Message)

Much like the Athenians, you might recognize a lacking in your life or a need for something to bring it definition, meaning, and purpose, but mistakenly opt for something that is insufficient for what you need it to do or be.

That's right, there are a number of *false gods* that populate the campus culture and vie for your attention and allegiance. And they're already present on campus in the form of opportunities and experiences that you might encounter regularly throughout a typical day. What happens is the Enemy begins to magnify your struggle, and then subtly suggests that you might feel better if you would just spend some time doing "X."

And before you know it, "X" has become an idol, a false god in your life.

Yep, it's just that simple.

And what I hope to do within the pages of this book is expose some of the most alluring idols around campus—idols that capture the hearts and minds of countless students each year—and reveal how they pale in comparison to the One True God.

How it's impacting you now

You are in the midst of a major life transition. Your priorities, passions, character, and purpose are all still taking shape. You're not who you were when you graduated from high school, but you're not yet a finished product either. You're a work in progress, and that can be a tough place to live.

Because so much of this transition is tied to your core identity, you'll need God to be central in your life. If He's not, you'll undoubtedly struggle to see and understand a lot of what's around you (at least in the right ways). When God is not central, the Enemy often seizes the opportunity to put one of his false gods in that key position. When that happens, chaos inevitably follows.

If you're like many students who follow false gods, your relationships are likely self-serving and without appropriate boundaries. Maybe not all of them, but you might be surprised at how true this is for many of your relationships. In some instances you're using other people; in other instances, you're allowing yourself to be used. You're establishing unhealthy relational habits and patterns. You're reinforcing any trust issues already present.

Your education may likely be seen as a necessary means to a one-dimensional, self-serving end in the form of a big payday. You're getting the degree necessary to win you that well-paying job that will yield you the kind of comfortable lifestyle that you've come to believe life is all about. It's the most immediate hoop you must jump through on your way to earning your slice of the American Dream.

Your priorities may be (yep, you guessed it) focused on you and your needs. *What feels good right now? What can I get away with? How can I manipulate this situation such that I get the most, while giving up the least? How do I make this a "win" for me?* You may not be consciously thinking these things, but if you stopped to examine your actions and attitudes, you might be able to see the connection. Little, if any, consideration is being given towards others.

And then there's your purpose in life. This will be the hardest thing to make sense of, if you really stop to think about it, because if you're like most students who follow false gods, living in the little world you've created (where everything is about you), there will be very little that speaks at all to purpose beyond self-gratification and self-glorification. Other than the amassing of more and more possessions, power, influence, or fame, you will struggle to comprehend the point of life—which will eventually make it a very real struggle.

But it doesn't have to be this way.

Read that again—*it does not have to be this way!*

Yet, before we explore the hope that can be found in an alternative way of understanding your identity, let's explore where you might find yourself if you don't make some intentional decisions about who you want to be and Whose you want to be, and knowingly continue to follow any number of false gods.

The long-term damage of following false gods

The longer you struggle to understand your true identity as a child of God, the more malformed your identity will become.

Why?

Because you become what you worship, what you follow. Something is shaping you. Something is serving as your god. And if it's not the God of the universe, then it's something that is distorting the "you" that God desires for you to become.

And it doesn't just impact your present, but your future as well. The ways of thinking and believing that you adopt during your formative college years will shape in you a way of understanding and living that will last long after you graduate.

The ways in which you relate to others, approach your work, prioritize your life, and understand your purpose in life will be broken. Instead of being shaped by God, they will be shaped by some lesser god that has been given authority in your life—by you!

This will, in turn, cause you to live in ways that are harmful to you, inconsiderate of others, and unpleasing to God.

Can change happen? Is it possible?

Yes. Of course.

But college is a time when habits get shaped, patterns take form, and memories get seared into your mind, and collectively they make a certain way of life both natural and easy. As creatures of habit who also like things that are natural and easy, it may be very hard to change.

I don't mean to be an alarmist, but this is important stuff. So if this book is causing the alarms in your heart and mind to sound, it was worth the time it took for me to write it—and you to read it.

False gods just can't compare

When we try to liken any false god with the One True God, we find that there's really no comparison.

On the one hand, there are the false gods that we see depicted here in Psalm 115 as the handiwork of humans:

> *Their idols are silver and gold, the work of human hands. They have mouths, but do not speak; eyes, but do not see. They have ears, but do not hear; noses, but do not smell. They have hands, but do not feel; feet, but do not walk; and they do not make a sound in their throat. Those who make them become like them; so do all who trust in them.* (Psalm 115:4–8 ESV)

Why would we worship something, *anything* really, that we could conceive of with our minds or build with our hands?

That seems backwards. Shouldn't it—the created thing—worship us? Or at the very least, follow us?

Reread the last sentence of that passage from Psalms: "Those who make them become like them; so do all who trust in them."

Those who make idols become like them.
So do all who trust in idols.

This reality is what makes the decision about *Who* we follow so significant and *what* we trust in, so important!

By comparison, consider the truth about the one true, living God and how a life of following Jesus differs from following false gods:

> *Whenever, though, they turn to face God as Moses did, God removes the veil and there they are—face-to-face! They suddenly recognize that God is a living, personal presence, not a piece of chiseled stone. And when God is personally present, a living Spirit, that old, constricting legislation is recognized as obsolete. We're free of it! All of us! Nothing between us and God, our faces shining with the brightness of his face. And so we are transfigured much like the Messiah, our lives gradually becoming brighter and more beautiful as God enters our lives and we become like him.* (2 Corinthians 3:16–18 THE MESSAGE)

The veil is lifted.
We see God, as Moses did, face-to-face.
We are free.
We gradually become more like Him.
Wow!

God's desire to redeem and restore you

As we get further into the pages of this book, don't be surprised if you find that you've been misled and have even strayed after a false god or two. The truth is, we've all been there at one point or another.

We're all susceptible to being led astray at any given point in time, but our best defense is having a growing awareness of the false gods that look for ways to gain our attention and, eventually, our allegiance—and how they just can't compare to the One True God.

As we're exposed to any truth, we are faced with one of two options:

1. We go on living like we previously had, as if we do not believe or do not care about what we have learned,

or

2. We make a change. We discern how this new truth is meant to influence and shape our existence, and we allow change or we help to facilitate change into our lives.

The choice is ultimately ours to make.

God will not force us to do anything.

But God is always at work, lovingly attempting to win us over and knowing full well that what He has to offer us is so, so much more than anything or anyone else.

>>

The truth is, I'd much rather be talking with you face-to-face, having a series of conversations over coffee or some other beverage, taking our time over the course of many weeks and months to explore the issues you're facing in college, and talking in a context where we could bat around ideas, think through personal challenges, and talk about the reality of what you're seeing and experiencing on campus.

But unless you happen to attend the school I work at, this likely won't happen. So I'm writing this book to warn you about what I'm seeing on numerous campuses and to encourage you to choose wisely—to choose God.

I'm writing because I don't think you'll see many of the pitfalls that lay before you (at least, not for what they really are) unless someone points them out. Like I said, we have an Enemy who is cunning and deceptive. This means that the destructive things that lay in wait for you will likely not look very harmful in appearance, much like the fruit of the Tree of Good and Evil that Adam and Eve took for themselves, even after God had warned them not to. You will be tempted in a variety of ways by things that will appear harmless, but could all too easily become idols that derail your present and destroy your future.

I write because I care.

And I'm not alone. There are a lot of older adults, maturing followers of Jesus, that care about you and how you navigate your formative college years. And I hope you'll seek out one of them! Look around your campus or step into a local church, they're there. And they want to help you succeed in life!

I'm letting you know right now that you might not like some of what I have to say in the chapters to come. So let me reiterate now: *I care about you and your future.*

I was once a young-in-my-faith Christian trying to navigate the challenges and temptations of college life. And I'm thankful for everyone and everything that God used to make those years some of the most significant of my life. Now I'm a pastor to college students.

I'm also a dad to five small children. And if for some reason I was unable to talk to my own kids about what we will explore in this book, I would hope that someone else would be willing to sit and have a number of honest, heart-to-heart conversations with each of them. The kinds of conversations that this book will hopefully make you want to have because the subject matter is incredibly important. I see too many students giving themselves to the false gods that are so prevalent around campus.

You may not see the harm. Or if you do, you may be so entangled with it that you now find yourself feeling stuck. Feeling trapped.

And when we're trapped long enough, hope has a way of fading. Are you there yet? Do you know what I'm talking about?

When hope fades, the painful trap that we have been ensnared by becomes home, where we concede to spend the rest of our days.

But you deserve better than that. I think so and, more important, God thinks so.

I'm going to point out some of the dangers I see and to identify the short-term consequences of engaging with these false gods because they have long-term ramifications.

I want you to see the hope that is available to you now in the saving and restorative work of Jesus.

Yes, the choices you make now will not only have immediate effects, but implications for your future. Those choices will eventually shape (or even dictate) your path—both the successes and the failures. So if you're interested in thriving during your college years, and the life you will lead long after you leave college, then I encourage you to read on!

My prayer is that you will heed the warnings I share and step into the life-giving grace that Jesus offers. As you do, I encourage you to bring others along with you and assist those around you who are unknowingly winding their way down a very destructive path with little, if any, awareness of what they are doing.

Now matters.

The choices you make count.

Don't allow yourself to be deceived by the Deceiver any longer. He doesn't care about you. His only interests lie in seeing you make a mess of your life, while believing that you're "fine," and that how you live now doesn't really make a difference.

Hear me say that there is Truth in our world and a Truth-teller who cares a great deal about you. His interests lie in seeing you make the most of your life—the life He has given to you.

So what do you say? Are you ready to expose the idols around campus that beg for your attention and eventual allegiance, to begin to live in light of *who* you are becoming, and *Whose* you really are?

Let's go!

EXPOSING THE CAMPUS GODS

THE gOD OF ACHIEVEMENT

Do not turn away after useless idols. They can do you no good, nor can they rescue you, because they are useless.

1 Samuel 12:21

Let me tell you a story about a former student of mine named Lucy.

I met Lucy late in her junior year. We crossed paths as I was walking back to my office after a campus event one evening.

Lucy was not doing so well.

We talked for quite a while there on the sidewalk—about what she was struggling with and how she had gotten to that empty, lonely, lost-feeling place.

You see, early on in Lucy's freshman year she was awakened to the plight of children in the impoverished country of Haiti. She struggled to believe that kids could be subjected to such horrible conditions, and she just knew deep down inside she needed to do something about it.

Lucy felt implicated. She had seen and experienced too much to just simply settle back into her comfortable life in America and do nothing to help bring about change.

So she had the brainstorm to create a movement on our campus. It was nothing too flashy or extreme, just a simple way for her peers to give money to help hurting kids in Haiti.

Well, it took off! Before long Lucy was receiving local media attention, assistance from the campus administration, financial support, a wide variety of other resources, and, of course, a lot of opinions about what she should do next. Things were starting to feel out of her control.

What had started as a simple desire to help kids had morphed into a burden that she felt compelled to carry. It was still helping to meet needs of those who couldn't help themselves, but she didn't like where it had taken her, nor how it was controlling her life.

The truth of the matter was that Lucy didn't really know who she was apart from this initiative anymore. And what was worse, she had otherwise aimlessly meandered her way through the first three years of her college education, burned a lot of relational bridges, missed out on a wide variety of campus opportunities and experiences that she had fully intended to explore during her college years, and even unknowingly wandered away from God. She confessed to me that she didn't like who she had become, in part, because she had let this great project become her entire life.

Lucy had succeeded on one hand; she had begun a movement that was providing aid to a hurting part of the world. But on the other hand, Lucy felt as though she was failing at the rest of her life. And the part that she was succeeding in, she didn't even like anymore.

She had become obsessed with the success of something meaningful and significant, because of the assistance that it could provide to others, but seemingly forgot about or neglected every other thing that was important or interesting in her life.

>>

It's probably not too hard to see how achievement would make the list of idols found on campus. So much of our growing-up years is focused on achieving in certain areas so that we might be happy, successful, and on our way to a comfortable life.

Our North American culture likes to talk in terms of winners and, subsequently, losers. And nobody wants to be a loser. This means that just about everyone is working towards being some sort of winner: in the classroom, within the team or club, and even in relationships.

Being a winner has been a driving motivation for many generations of young people. It's true of your generation as well.

Can you pinpoint its origin in your own life?

When did achieving begin to take priority for you? Why?

Were your parents the catalyst for getting you started on this path? If so, what do you think was behind it? Were their intentions pure? Did they simply want to see you learn and grow your way into your fullest potential? What parent *doesn't* want their kids to be successful?

And truthfully, what kid doesn't want to be their very best self?

Likewise, I believe this is what God wants for all of us. I think it's what He had in mind when He created you: you becoming the very best *you* possible.

But when achievement gets elevated to an improper place in one's life to a point where it begins to (mis)shape identity, (mis)form understanding, and (mis)direct one's path, then it becomes something it was never intended to be.

What I see on campus

I see a lot of students who are determined to do their very best at all costs. They want to be successful. They want to be a one-of-a-kind achiever. They want to be the leader of every group they're in, captain of every team they're on, and in control of every relationship and situation they find themselves in.

They simply want to be the best at *everything*!

And you know what? It's wrecking them.

Students like this struggle to be content in just about every situation, always believing there's something more, something *better* to be attained.

They see people and experiences as opportunities to help them climb some sort of academic, organizational, or relational ladder of success.

In the classroom they are less concerned with learning and much more concerned with making an "A." They don't care much for exploring the topic at hand (unless it's to prove they're right) and, instead, simply want to know: "Will this be on the exam?" They're consumers of information, for the sake of being able to pull it out (on the exam, in the debate, or in the paper), and often struggle to see how the content of the class is meant to shape their lives.

Around campus the achievement-obsessed student can be found trying to create the best possible scenario for themselves. They struggle to be content with simply being a participant in anything, and believe their time would be better spent in leadership. The idea of being led by someone else (especially a peer) is nearly unthinkable. If they cannot step into a leading role somewhere on campus, they'll likely attempt to create one for themselves or look for an opportunity off campus to exercise their need to lead.

Relationally speaking, the students dominated by a need to achieve will struggle greatly. Since they are most often trying to position themselves above others, they will struggle to celebrate the successes of those around them. They will often feel the need to be in control, which will quickly short-circuit most relationships, or, at the very least, keep them at a very shallow existence.

Does any of this sound familiar to you? Can you relate?

It's important to note that I'm not talking about *all* students who strive to do well and achieve great things. What I am talking about here are the students who are controlled by their need to

---

Some **Quick Facts** Related to Students and Achievement:

In one recent study among students sixteen to twenty-four years old:

- 82% said they believe the next Bill Gates is in their generation
- 51% said they believe they know the next Bill Gates
- 24% said they believe they are the next Bill Gates!*

A 2009 random sampling of students from different states, asking them what their goal was for after graduation, revealed:

- #1 goal: to get rich.
- #2 goal: to be famous.**

*Source: Tim Elmore's *Generation iY: Our Last Chance to Save Their Future*, (Poet Gardener Publishing, 2010), p. 41.

** Source: Tim Elmore's *Artificial Maturity: Helping Kids Meet the Challenge of Becoming Authentic Adults* (Jossey-Bass, 2012), p. 83.

achieve at the highest of levels, and see all of life through an achievement-oriented lens.

It's possible to be a high-achieving student without being controlled by it. But it's not necessarily easy.

How it's impacting you now

For the students who bow to the god of achievement, life is often far from enjoyable. Sure, there are moments of happiness, triumph, and even relief. But those feelings are fleeting, and often replaced with feelings of stress, fear, and anxiety.

For the students who struggle to control their need to achieve, stress becomes a constant companion. That stress often pushes them, constantly urging them to do more, and do it better. Serving the god of achievement is an unending task that cannot be completed or completely satisfied. While some stress can actually spur us on to good productivity, chronic stress can lead to a very unhealthy existence.

And one doesn't have to live with stress long before you suddenly realize that fear has joined the proverbial party. Fear has a way of creeping in through the back door of your life and setting up camp like an unwelcomed squatter. No one desires to live in a state of fear. But many students live with fear, especially the ceaseless achievers. And it's a fear of being outdone that will keep them awake at night, plotting their next three moves and not allowing room to trust anyone.

Fear, when full-blown, can be debilitating. Anxiety, the well-known associate of fear, can be found lurking in the dark corners of every campus, a constant resident in search of its next victim. There's really nothing positive that can be said about it. It's an illness that quite literally can bring one to a paralyzing standstill. It can be triggered by a wide variety of things (or nothing at all) and can render an individual utterly debilitated, to the point of being unable to function. This, of course, is an absolute nightmare for the student that follows the god of achievement.

The long-term damage of following the god of achievement

One of the lies the Enemy sells to us is that we are in control.

That we have the power to quit anything whenever we want.

That this god of achievement is really more of a power we can tap into when we need it, and then set it aside when we don't need it any longer.

But when we bow down to an idol long enough, we struggle to believe that there's anything else worthy of our time and allegiance. In the case of achievement, we believe that achieving—more and more—is the only thing that will bring us fulfillment. So we're tempted, therefore, to give in to it further. And when we do, we find ourselves more entrenched in the power and control of this false god than we were before. *And we're emptier, too.*

A life given to the pursuit of achievement above all else will eventually lead to a life that lacks some pretty significant things:

1. Contentment

The god of achievement will have you believing that what you've produced is OK, but that there's more to be done. There's more to possess. There's more to conquer. Seated deep within will be a restlessness that doesn't allow you even the slightest bit of peace, joy, or contentment—ever.

2. The belief that you're good enough

A prolonged lack of contentment will eventually bleed over from what you believe about your work, your position(s), and even your relationship(s), into your sense of self. The new lie will not only pertain to the things that you're a part of or the work you do, but to *you* as a human being. Instead of believing that you are loved and accepted as a child of God, you will waste vast amounts of time and energy striving to achieve your way to "good enough."

3. Significant and sustained relationships

The god of achievement will ultimately rob you of just about every relationship you have. Whether it's the demanding schedule and pace that you feel compelled to keep, or your inability to trust others and let them get close, relationships will be hard to come by. The god of achievement will cause you to see most everyone you encounter as someone who either is trying to outdo you, take something from you, or someone that can serve as a means to an end, a tool you can use or manipulate to get what you want. No matter how you look at it, this way of thinking and living is not conducive for healthy and long-lasting relationships.

As relational beings, we are not created to go through life on our own. And the Enemy knows this. So the god of achievement will continuously tempt you to believe that the only way to earn acceptance and approval is through producing, gaining, and achieving more and more, believing that people will then like you, but this ultimately serves to drive others away from (and not toward) you.

It's a bad place to get to.

And an even harder place to get out of.

But you don't have to get (or stay) stuck in this place.

You don't have to continue to serve the god of achievement!

There's just no comparison

The god of achievement feeds on our desire to be successful, to be respected—to make a difference in the world. This god twists and distorts our God-given desire to be a part of something significant and attempts to convince us that *we* can make ourselves significant through personal accomplishments.

And although his ways can be conniving and convincing, the god of achievement has little of significance to offer.

The One True God, the One who created us with a deep desire to live lives of meaning and purpose, wants us to live successful and fulfilling lives according to *His* standards, and not the world's.

And when we delve into the heart and mind of the One True living God and explore the nature of His plans for us, achievement is all over the place.

*"'For I know the plans I have for you,' declares the L*ORD*, 'plans to prosper you and not to harm you, plans to give you hope and a future'"* (Jer. 29:11). That's the heart of God for us.

"'Very truly I tell you, whoever believes in me will do the works I have been doing, and they will do even greater things than these, because I am going to the Father'" (John 14:12). That's the heart of God for us.

"'This is to my Father's glory, that you bear much fruit, showing yourselves to be my disciples'" (John 15:8). That's the heart of God for us.

"'But seek first his kingdom and his righteousness, and all these things will be added to you'" (Matt. 6:33 ESV). That's the heart of God for us.

The god of achievement says you are as good as your résumé. He wants you to become so obsessed with keeping it polished and up-to-date that you have little time or energy to give to things that matter.

Consider the apostle Paul, a crusader against early Christians, and his impressive first-century resume:

> *If someone else thinks they have reasons to put confidence in the flesh, I have more: circumcised on the eighth day, of the people of Israel, of the tribe of Benjamin, a Hebrew of Hebrews; in regard to the law, a Pharisee; as for zeal, persecuting the church; as for righteousness based on the law, faultless.* (Philippians 3:4–6)

All things that he thought to be of the utmost importance—until he encountered Jesus.

> *But whatever were gains to me I now consider loss for the sake of Christ. What is more, I consider everything a loss because of the surpassing worth of knowing Christ Jesus my Lord, for whose sake I have lost all things. I consider them garbage, that I may gain Christ and be found in him, not having a righteousness of my own that comes from the law, but that which is through faith in Christ—the righteousness that comes from God on the basis of faith.* (Philippians 3:7–9)

The One True God desires to shape our lives to achieve a kind of greatness that provides us the deepest satisfaction while giving God the greatest glory. Go with the God who promises "much fruit," "greater things," and true greatness in the only Kingdom that will endure. This God delivers.

Indeed, God wants us to be successful, to live lives of significance, to make a difference in the world. But it's success, significance, and making a difference by *His* standards, over and above the world's.

God's desire to redeem and restore you in this area

Is achievement an idol in your life? How about one of your friends?

Achievement and the desire to be successful is not a bad thing in and of itself.

Again, I think God longs for us to do our best and to be our very best self. But the desire to achieve needs to be kept in check and properly understood through the active work of God's Spirit in our life.

When we yield our life to God—and all that our life encompasses—achievement takes on a different look and feel altogether. In fact, the kinds of things that would be deemed worthy of achieving change completely.

In the classroom the shift moves from a grade to learning. From how this class will affect your GPA to how it will prepare you to make a difference in the world. From being annoyed with the work to seeing it as an opportunity to be further trained and equipped for Kingdom work.

In leadership positions the shift moves from a title to an opportunity. From feeling like you've arrived as a leader to humbly knowing that you've been given a chance to learn, while leading others. From seeing it as one more thing to pad your resume to discerning how this opportunity can further prepare you for the work that God wants you to commit your life to.

And in relationships the shift moves from hunting for your next friend or significant other to prayerfully discerning who to spend time with, and why. From quickly moving on when the excitement fades or there's the least bit of conflict to learning the significance of commitment and perseverance within meaningful relationships. From thinking about what a relationship can do for you to learning more about what you can bring into a relationship.

Achievement isn't a bad thing, in and of itself.

But it's not meant to be the guiding force in our lives. When we elevate achievement to an unhealthy, godlike status in our lives, we become someone that we were never intended to be.

Responding to God's invitation

Let's revisit Lucy's story.

She and I continued to meet regularly during the remainder of her junior year, primarily to talk about how she could bring much-needed change to her current situation (having started a movement to help kids hurting in Haiti, only to see it grow and evolve into something big and successful, but overwhelming and out of her control).

She didn't want to shut the whole thing down, but she knew she didn't want to continue to invest so much of her time, energy, and effort into it either.

So we contrived a plan for building a leadership culture within the movement, while also making a way for her to slowly remove herself from her involvement within it.

After successfully phasing herself out of the movement she had dreamed up, Lucy went on to have an incredible senior year, doing all of the things she had planned to do all along.

She also graduated and returned to her work in Haiti—and various other parts of the world—bringing love and assistance to those who were most in need of it.

>>

Achievement is a powerful force.

But God is *so* much bigger!

And He wants so much more for you than a great GPA, a laundry list of unfulfilling leadership positions, a padded resume, and a record of shallow or broken relationships. God wants you to grow, mature, and develop in a whole host of ways. God wants you to be successful by His standards, much more so than the world's. He wants you to learn, lead, and love well.

But this will require that you look to Him, and trust Him with *who* you are and *how* you are. You need to be willing to let go of your desire to achieve, control, and master the people and experiences you encounter.

This is much easier said than done, but achievement will not satisfy nor fulfill what you long for most in life: unconditional love and acceptance.

So here are some steps you might consider as you look to yield control of this area of your life to God:

* Ask God to show you the way(s) that achievement has become an idol in your life.
* Ask God to give you a better understanding of achievement, and what it means to do and be your best.
* Ask God to help you release the need to be in control and/or on top.
* Ask God to assist you in repairing any damage the god of achievement has done in your relationships.
* Ask God to empower and equip you to come alongside others who are following this god of achievement and help them to see how much more can be gained through a life with God.
* Ask God to reveal to you some people in your life that it would be beneficial to begin living intentionally with. Seek out peers who can encourage, pray for, and hold you accountable in this area—as you do the same for them. Also find a mentor, someone older and wiser that you might be able to spend regular time with, learning to better understand God's desire for your life.

* At the end of each of chapter, be willing to sit patiently, in silence, as you make these requests to God and listen for a response or leading.
* Trust that God wants to do a new work in you, as well as use you in the lives of others.

THE gOD OF FREEDOM

You, my brothers and sisters, were called to be free. But do not use your freedom to indulge the flesh; rather, serve one another humbly in love.

Galatians 5:13

Koby and I met not long into his spring semester on campus.

Koby seemed like a lot of the students I've met during my years of working on campus: excited about life, *not* so excited about homework, thankful for great friends, and hopeful about the future.

What I would later learn about Koby was that he was actually sent home halfway through his first semester for drug possession on campus. He was suspended for the remainder of that term, with no promise of being able to return to campus once he had served his time.

As we got to know each other over the course of that spring term, Koby revealed to me that upon arriving on campus he quickly found himself in over his head. He was without a lot of the boundaries he had grown up with (and had unknowingly taken for granted), and began to explore the limits of his newfound freedom.

Before he knew it, he was rarely attending his classes, sleeping most of the day, staying out all night, drinking, and experimenting with drugs, and completely neglecting why he was there in the first place—to get an education.

His life hit a crossroads in October of his freshman year, when the dorm resident assistant happened to smell something "strange" emanating from his dorm room. One thing led to another and his room was searched, exposing his possession and new habit, and gaining him a one-way ticket home for the remainder of the fall term.

He described the feelings of personal failure, letting his parents down, and being embarrassed in front of his friends and hall mates as he was removed from campus in handcuffs, as things he would like never to repeat again. He also described the two and a half months he subsequently spent at home—attempting to regain his parents' trust, attending regular counseling sessions and Narcotics Anonymous meetings, and having to explain to those who thought he was off at college why he was now back home—as months he would rather forget.

Koby had never intended to go off to college and have his first semester unfold the way that it did. In fact, Koby had never intended to hit the party scene or be anything less than a fully committed and successful student.

But he allowed his newfound freedom to quickly become a god in his life, and it wreaked havoc while it was given the chance to reign supreme.

>>

Can you relate to Koby and his struggle with new freedoms?

Is your story anything like his? Do you have any friends like Koby?

One of the hallmarks of the college experience is getting the chance to move out of your parents' house (unless you happen to be commuting from home) and experience some new freedoms.

And this is a good thing, because it is meant to assist you with your transition from adolescence to adulthood. Since most colleges and universities have requirements for first-year students to live on campus (if they're not living at home), the campus context becomes a quasi–controlled environment for this new kind of freedom to be explored.

There are resident assistants (RAs) and resident directors (RDs) who do their best to make sure that you are looked after and, if necessary, they're there to step in and let you know when you exceed the bounds of your freedom (at least within the residence halls).

New freedoms extend into the campus eateries as well, where most new students must have a meal plan. Most meal plans give students some options for where they can eat, and most eateries have menus that have a wide assortment of both healthy and not-so-healthy options. So a student could opt to eat nutritiously and responsibly at every meal; but they could also choose to eat cereal and ice cream at every meal, and no one would likely step in to object.

Most terms, students are given the chance to select what classes they will take, when they will take them, and who they will take them with—until, of course, they choose a major. Then, they're fortunate if they are still able to select what time they'd like to take a class, as well as whom they might take it from.

And then there are campus security officers who are strategically situated around campus to make sure that no one's exploration of their new freedoms puts anyone else in harm's way.

Controlled freedom. Flexible boundaries.

But other than these few instances, college students living on campus have a lot of freedom and free time, which sets the stage for students to have to make some pretty significant choices about:

* How you will wield your freedom.
* Whether or not you'll go to class.
* Whether or not you'll do your homework.
* Who you'll spend your time with—and what you'll do.
* Decisions about sex, drugs, alcohol, and the stereotypical college party scene.

Some **Quick Facts** Related to Students and How They Spend Their Time:

- Facebook users in college spend 1–5 hours a week studying, while non-users spend 11–15 hours a week studying.
- Students spend 24.5 hours a week e-mailing, instant messaging, and web surfing.
- College students spend an average of 10.2 hours a week drinking.
- Males in college report having more than twice as much free time as females—9 hours a week for men, 4 for women.

Source: Infographic found at http://tinyurl.com/ladguqk, provided by GuideToOnlineSchools.com.

Infographic provided by: GuideToOnlineSchools.com.

* Your faith and involvement in faith-forming activities and communities—like going to church *or not*, making friends with other believers *or not*, and finding a place to serve *or not*.

The choices you have related to the new freedoms you are getting the chance to experience are meant to serve as a way of helping you grow and mature into a healthy and responsible young adult.

But increasingly this is not the case for a growing percentage of students.

What I see on campus

I see a lot of students who embrace the newfound freedoms that come with moving off to college, but resist the corresponding responsibilities that naturally come with those new freedoms.

It's a season of life that's been defined by different psychologists and sociologists as "emerging adulthood," or "delayed adulthood," or "prolonged adolescence." No matter how you label it, it's a season of life that's marked by young people taking longer and longer to "grow up." They want all of the rights adults have, but the accountability levels of youth. They want to enjoy freedom, but not the responsibility that might come with it.

And if you don't feel like this is painting a very favorable picture of this season of life . . . well, you're right.

Truth be told, it's not all the fault of the student.

At some level parents may be partly to blame because they've not exposed their children to new levels of freedom (and the corresponding responsibilities) before they go off to college. And this was not likely a malicious decision (or even a conscious one) on their part. In fact, it was probably just the opposite; they were trying to create a comfortable life that was favorable for their child's success.

Likewise, institutions (such as the high school you graduated from and the university you now attend) have, to varying degrees, bought into the consumerist nature of our culture and chosen to make the college experience more and more about students and student desires rather than creating a context in which students could be exposed to uncomfortable situations and scenarios that serve to grow, educate, and mature them. The goal of institutions like these has become to give students, as the consumers, the happiest possible experience. They want each one to love their involvement, take pride in their education, stay for the duration of their degree, tell all their friends they should also attend, and ultimately become a fruitful (and giving) alum.

And then there is *you*. Yes, you as a student have a part in this as well. You have choices to make regarding whether or not you will step into some of the responsibilities that present themselves alongside newfound freedoms.

More often than not, I see students choosing to opt out of these responsibilities. Some students plead ignorant, even if they're not. Some students get their parents to take care of it, even though they should take care of it themselves. Some students get their parents to pay for it, even though they could. Some students get someone else to do the work, and suffer as a result.

And what I ultimately see on campus is a growing gap between those who use their freedom wisely and live into new levels of responsibility and those who do not.

The gap is widening, and the number of students on the good side of this gap is shrinking.

How it's impacting you now

As with many of the false gods that are addressed in this book, there doesn't seem to be any noticeable harm being done in the moment.

You're having fun enjoying your freedoms and casting responsibility to the wind but, whether you know it or not, it's costing you.

As I've previously mentioned, these are some of the most formative years of your life—years that you cannot get back—and if you fail to use them well, then you're simply out of luck.

It's not that it's impossible to learn these lessons later in life and take corrective actions at that point. But *how* you think and *what* you think about—the priorities you set and the ways you choose to live during your formative college years—will all serve to shape who you become and how you will view and live in the world.

If you're not living intentionally during your college years, then you're missing out on some great opportunities to be shaped and formed during a season of life that has the potential to mean the most for your future.

The long-term damage of following the god of freedom

The god of freedom has a way of embedding itself deep in our psyche, giving us a growing sense that we've got life all figured out and planting a spirit of suspicion and resistance toward anyone who might try to tell us otherwise.

Over the course of time, one could easily become a glutton for freedom: doing what one wants, when one wants, and rebelling against anything that might attempt to hinder one (like a boss, a mate, or responsibilities of most any kind). People like this will be difficult to employ, hard to be around, and unreliable to most everyone they come into contact with.

But you won't care, because the god of freedom will convince you that *those* people and things aren't worth your time and don't really care about you or your well-being. *They're trying to keep you down, control you, or steal your freedom.* And the god of freedom won't stand for that. The god of freedom believes you need to be free to soar.

No attachments.

No restrictions.

No responsibilities.

You could become skeptical and cynical of systems, structures, and the powers that be. It will be hard to see the positive in any of these things, because the god of freedom will impair your vision such that you're only able to see how they are infringing upon your rights and liberties. You will set yourself against the powers of this world—including God. You'll see yourself as a defender of freedom, but in reality you'll be seen by most everyone as an extremist without a clear grasp on reality.

Ultimately, you have the potential to render yourself ineffective in most realms of life. Other people won't know how to relate to or trust you. And the freedom that you had fought so hard to protect and maintain will become a prison that keeps you isolated from, and irrelevant in, the world in which you live.

There's just no comparison

I love the story of the prodigal son.

It is a beautiful picture of so much of life: the brash arrogance that youth can engender, the competitive pursuit of fairness (which often translates into making sure we're not forgotten and that we "get ours"), and the gracious understanding of the seasoned elder who was once a youth himself.

As the story goes, the younger of two sons decided that he was ready to leave home and explore the big, big world on his own and on his terms.

Well, not much time passed before the young man had squandered away all of the money he had been given by his father (one-third of his father's estate), and he found himself homeless and hungry without any way of meeting his most basic needs.

His freedom had not yielded all that he had expected.

So the son returns home with all the rewards of his freedom, the "gifts" of the god of freedom:

* Rags for clothes.
* Worn-out shoes.
* Halfway starving to death.
* Filled with regret, self-hate, and worthlessness.
* Ready to submit to live in the slave quarters.
* Forfeiting his identity as his father's son.

This is what the god of freedom delivers; it literally exiles you to slavery.

But the One True God gives gifts beyond anything we might imagine. Hear the heart of God for us in the acts of the father from the story of the prodigal son.

* The father stands out at the end of the driveway and *searches* the horizon for the form of his lost son.
* In an act of throwing aside his own status, the father runs to greet his prodigal son.

* The father throws his arms around his prodigal son and embraces him.
* The father kisses his son.
* The father calls for the best robe to be put on his son.
* The father orders a ring to be put on his son's finger.
* The father gets new sandals for his son's feet.
* The father has a fattened calf killed and declares a festival celebration.

This is the heart of God for us—even for those of us who have left Him in search of our own freedom.

God's desire to redeem and restore you in this area

Freedom is a good thing, a *very* good thing. In fact, that's what Christ came to do: set us free. When Jesus said, "I have come that [you] may have life, and have it to the full" (John 10:10), *freedom* is what He was talking about. He came to earth, lived thirty-three years, suffered a sacrificial death, overcame death, and went back to the right hand of God in order that we might be free and experience all that life has to offer.

Our problem is that instead of loving the Giver of the good gift of freedom, we have decided to love the gift instead. The god of freedom, just like all of the other false gods, is a god that has the capacity to get its claws dug deep into our flesh during our formative college years, such that it sidetracks us from the future God has in mind for us.

God desires to redeem this gift of freedom for us.

He doesn't want to control us, or how we use our freedom. Instead, He hopes that we'll use this gift in ways that honor Him. God wants us to live in freedom, not become a slave to it. He wants it to be a beautiful way of life, not an idol that warps everything else that it touches.

But for those of us who choose to yield our lives to God and follow in the ways of Jesus, there will be a cost. Truth be told, there will be a cost no matter whom we choose to follow. But the cost of following Christ comes in the form of responsibility. And while God will ask for us to render our freedom back over to Him, He won't make us give it up or even turn His back on us if we choose to withhold it. He wants us to choose to give Him control of our life. Freely.

As we do, God will grow us and bless us in ways we never would have imagined. And as we yield control of our freedom to God, we'll be surprised by how free we actually find ourselves!

Responding to God's invitation

Let's revisit Koby's story.

As I previously mentioned, after being suspended for drug possession during his first semester on campus, he returned the following spring.

He was thankful for the opportunity to be back and for the warm welcome he received from his friends. But as long as I knew Koby, he seemed to live under a shroud of shame from having embarrassed himself and let down his parents that first semester on campus. He knew in his mind that his parents (and God) had forgiven him, but he seemed to struggle to believe that he wasn't forever labeled a screwup.

We talked from time to time throughout the remainder of his years on campus, but as far as I could tell, the reality of God's grace and forgiveness was never allowed to pass from Koby's head to his heart. He held on to the residue of a season of uninhibited freedom that was allowed to have its way, even for just a short time.

I hope that since we've last connected, things have changed for Koby, and I'm quite certain that God continues to try to get this message of love, grace, and acceptance through to him.

>>

I love that God never forces Himself on us.

He always gives us the choice to choose Him, or not.

But let's be clear here: We *all* serve someone (or something). And I contend that if we're not serving God, then we're serving a lesser god—a *false* god—that is ultimately controlled by an Enemy that cares nothing for us.

God wants to see you live life freely. God wants you to grow and mature in ways that responsibly use the freedom you've been blessed with. God wants you to work with Him to discern how best to live into the freedoms you've been afforded.

So, strangely, even paradoxically, in order to really and truly be free, we need to be willing to subject our freedom to the leading of God's Spirit. We need to be willing to give up our freedom in order to follow in the ways of Jesus. We need to surrender our ability to make decisions free and clear, without any consideration for anyone or anything else, in order to create room for God to show us what He might want.

It requires that we once again lay down our false gods before the One True God.

So here are some steps you might consider as you work to yield control of this area of your life to God:

* Ask God to reveal to you the way(s) that freedom has become an idol in your life.
* Ask God to prepare your heart and mind to understand freedom in some different ways.
* Ask God to help you to willingly (even joyfully) give your freedoms over to Him, in order that you may be *truly* free.
* Ask God to reveal to you the ways that following the false god of freedom has served to damage relationships in your life, and then ask Him to help you reconcile those relationships.
* Ask God to repair in you the way(s) in which the god of freedom has impaired your capacity to trust people, systems, and structures, and to give you a vision for how you might think of them, and even utilize and/or contribute to them.
* Ask God to help you know how to make the best use of your new freedoms such that He is glorified and you are used to make a positive impact in your campus, local, and global communities.
* Ask God to help you identify some peers who will pray for you, encourage you, and hold you accountable in this area of your life.
* Likewise, ask God to help you identify a mentor on or near campus (if you don't have one already), someone who can help you think through choices as they relate to the freedoms you're being exposed to.

THE gOD OF STATUS

For by the grace given me I say to every one of you:
Do not think of yourself more highly than you ought,
but rather think of yourself with sober judgment,
in accordance with the faith God has distributed to each of you.

Romans 12:3

Anna and I met one spring break while participating on a mission trip that went out from our campus.

One evening, while sitting around a big table in the basement of the church we were staying in, Anna and I began talking. And I was blindsided by what I learned.

Anna was a second semester junior who was getting involved with us—with anything ministry-related, really—for the first time since she'd arrived on campus as a freshman. Yet, a big part of the reason she chose to go to this particular school was because of the faith-forming opportunities it was going to afford her.

When I pushed her for more information, she confessed that she had simply gotten caught up in doing too many other things. She rushed for a sorority during her first year, and once accepted, felt the need to quickly fit in with her new friends—believing she needed to look, think, and act a certain way. She felt obligated to get involved with certain things and *avoid* others. She soon realized that few of the people she now claimed as "sisters" shared the vibrant faith she held.

It wasn't like she walked away from her faith, she explained, but more so that she didn't give it the time and attention it needed to grow and flourish.

She would go on to spend much of her sophomore and junior years focused on running in the right circles, pursuing prominent leadership roles, and doing everything that would raise her level of credibility, status, and influence within her sorority as well as the greater campus community.

And then something happened inside her one fateful day, not long before our spring break encounter. She saw a poster on campus describing one of the spring break opportunities, and she just knew in her heart that she needed to be on that trip.

So she signed up and came—*by herself.*

Yes, by herself.

I couldn't believe it. In part because, by everything I had observed on that trip, it seemed as though she was longtime friends with the majority of people on the team.

Not true. It turns out she didn't know a single person on the team before showing up to leave for our destination. Sure, she had seen a few of the team members around campus, but she had never talked to any of them before.

I was shocked.

What a bold move.

And it was at that point that some of the other voices around the table began to chime in to our conversation.

As it turned out, Anna's story was very similar to almost everyone on the team.

While some of the specifics differed, many of the stories echoed a neglect of the faith they had come to campus with as they pursued other more popular and/or profitable opportunities and experiences.

One by one they seemed to express similar feelings of relief, freedom, and true self in their choice to be there on that trip, albeit with no one they really knew. And for the first time in a long time they all seemed to express a level of pride and confidence in their decision to go against the social grain they'd been so caught up with, to do something (like a mission trip) that better fit with their deep-seated priorities and desires.

And that may very well have been the thing that grew such a quick and tight bond amongst our team.

>>

Starting at a young age, we begin to pick up on social structures and power positions. We see people of significance and we want to be like them. We see popular people and we want to be with them. We see beautiful people and we want to look like them.

We also see people who appear to be overlooked or who easily blend into the backdrop of life—and we know deep down that we *don't* want to be like that.

Much of this we pick up on at a subconscious level. And our desire to hold status that affords us popularity, power, influence, and attention begins to shape how we think and who we want to become.

And by the time you get to campus, you've likely gone through more than a few scenarios in which you were either on the good side of the status equation—or not. Late elementary school, middle school, and high school would have been the stomping grounds for this kind of power struggle and jockeying for social positions to take place. Sports teams would likely have been another. Performance groups, Boy Scouts, Girl Scouts, and even youth groups would also have been places where the god of status might have begun to plant seeds.

And if your family ever moved, then you likely would have gone through all of these struggles again.

The god of status is relentless in his attempts to convince you that you need to be the most beautiful, most popular, most liked person in any room, at all times. You'll find yourself constantly assessing the room, trying to discern who the smartest, best looking, funniest, or best leader might be. And if it's not you, your quest will be to figure out how to win the crowd into your overwhelming favor.

College, in many ways, is a chance to start over. A clean slate. A new community of people, in a new context, during a new season of life. And depending upon how deeply the god of status has worked in your life up to this point, there could very well be an even greater emphasis placed upon the importance of status as you settle into life on campus. *This is the chance you've been waiting for*, says the god of status. *This is your big break. You've learned some things from your past failures* (and/or successes, but he'll likely play to the insecurities that have been exposed by your failures), *and now is your time to shine. You deserve this. Don't let anyone tell you otherwise.*

And so you begin to strategize (consciously and subconsciously) about how to take your new community by storm.

How do I look? How do I fit in? What do I need to work on?
Who do I need to be friends with? Who can I get on "my team"?
Who do I need to keep my eye on; who is my competition?
What do I need to get involved in? And how can I take the lead?
What's going to get me seen?
How can I work things in my favor?
How can I eliminate those things that hinder me?

And just like that, the god of status can have you fixated on yourself and making your formative years all about *you*.

Do you know what I mean? Do you see this unfolding on your campus? In your social circles? Or in your own life?

I want you to know that life is about so much more than how you look and the kind of contrived status and struggle for power that the world tries to tell us is so important. While it's hard to see during your college years, these pursuits are ultimately a fruitless use of your time, energy, and efforts—a reality that the god of status wants you to never understand.

What I see on campus

I see a lot of mental and emotional energy being invested in the pursuit of status. The pursuit of image.

> Some **Quick Facts** about College Students and Social Involvements:
>
> - Today's students are much more withdrawn from the public square and more submerged in interpersonal relationships.
> - Few are involved in community organizations or other social change-oriented groups or movements.
> - Not many care to know much of substance about political issues and world events.
> - Few are intellectually engaged in any of the major cultural and ethical debates and challenges facing US society.
> - They are deeply invested in social life beyond their immediate selves—primarily through their interpersonal relationships.
> - Much of their lives appears to be centered on creating and maintaining personal relationships.
> - Managing personal relationships turns out for many to be not a distinct task reserved for routinely scheduled times of the day or week, but rather a ubiquitous, 24/7 life activity.
>
> Source: Christian Smith with Patricia Snell, *Souls in Transition: The Religious & Spiritual Lives of Emerging Adults* (Oxford University Press, 2009), p. 73–74.

Students are choosing to focus a lot of their time and attention on trying to say and do the right things, look the right way, be seen with the right people, position themselves in all the right ways, and ultimately set the stage in ways that will place them in the center—in the spotlight—hoping to gain them the attention, affection, and allegiance of every onlooker.

These students want to be idolized by their peers, desired by their counterparts, pursued by those with opportunities, and sought out for friendship, wisdom, and counsel of just about every kind.

They want to feel important—significant, even.

It's a very self-centered existence.

And all of this means that there is a lot of emphasis being put on the wrong things.

Instead of finding ways to reach out to others and lift up those who need assistance or look for ways to make the overall community a better, more thriving place to be—your life can become all about finding your sweet spot and leaving your mark. And it's not that finding your sweet spot or leaving a mark is a bad thing, but there are very different motivational factors that can lead to the same end.

The student who's enmeshed with the god of status wants to be loved by all and never forgotten. They want to be seen as the ideal in every capacity possible and highly pursued. They want the power and control that can come with a glamorous image and high social status on campus. They want to be able to shape relationships and environments to suit their own needs and desires.

Again, life becomes all about "*me.*"

All of which leads to growing levels of insecurity, because there can only be one "top dog."

The god of status makes sure that you're never content with who you are, what you look like, or where you are in life, and makes you feel like you constantly need to be looking for every opportunity to improve yourself and move your way up the social chain—while also paying close attention to those who might be looking to knock you down and take your place.

During a season of life when you should begin to feel more comfortable within your own skin and more confident in the person you are and are becoming (as it pertains to your unique gifts, talents, and passions), the god of status strives to get you increasingly fixated on where you stand, and how you look, in comparison to everyone else, much like your middle school and high school existence. Instead of growing up, you're being duped into believing that status is paramount.

How it's impacting you now

The god of status, like all other false gods and idols that we can become consumed with, has a way of messing with our heads. It has a way of mixing up our perception of what's important—and why. So, during your highly formative college years, you could potentially spend way too much of your time concerned with your looks, your body, what people think of you, what you can do to change their opinions and win them over, and/or how you might leverage things to eliminate them from, or dominate them within, the social and/or structural equation.

Instead of growing in your understanding of how God has made you—and your God-given gifts, talents, and passions—in ways that will naturally cause you to develop and blossom into the person God dreams for you to become, you might be tempted to manipulate and manufacture something fake.

Instead of seeing the good in other people and the potential for meaningful relationships, you could easily become skeptical of others' motives, while at the same time trying to figure out how they can help you in your quest for power, position, and influence. You could become a user and abuser of those around you because you increasingly see them as a means to an end.

You could also become overly obsessed with things like appearance, body image, leadership opportunities, popular opinion, and social circles. You could find yourself doing things for the wrong reasons. Exercise and how you eat won't be for health-related reasons, but solely focused on your appearance (which is often when eating disorders and/or an obsession with exercise can develop or further manifest itself). Leadership positions won't be seen as opportunities to serve your peers, the institution you attend, or organization you lead, but rather to build your reputation, grow your social clout, pad your resume, and set you up for future opportunities on campus and in the world. Your concern with popular opinion will have less to do with what people need (and how you might help meet those needs), and instead focus on how you can leverage that opinion to serve your interests. And socially speaking, you'll always be pressing towards the top of the social scene, while constantly suspicious of those around you.

In the end, your college experience will be reduced to a great big game of "king of the hill"—and you will have missed out on some great relationships, possibilities, and experiences along the way.

Why? Because the god of status will have your priorities and perceptions (about self, others, and life in general) all out of whack.

And you'll feel isolated from any kind of help, because the kind of people that will love you for who you are (and not what you have to offer them), won't find themselves playing this same game of king of the hill (or at least not for very long). The kind of people who can help you to become the man or woman that God wants you to be will work hard to avoid the trappings of the god of status.

If you don't make changes now, the future connected to following this false god does not hold much promise.

The long-term damage of following the god of status

You'll become shallow. Yep. I said it. And it's true. The long-term effects of being obsessed with status and image will be that you fail to focus on things that really matter in life.

Instead of tending to matters that will grow your faith, build your character, strengthen your integrity, and enlighten your sense of purpose in the world, your life will always be about you—how you appear, what others think of you, what you've done, and why people should want to be with you (or like you, or want to follow you).

The god of status is a very demanding god and won't leave you time for anything of real substance or worth. You'll be confined to a life of self-absorption, self-promotion, and endless self-improvement. Body issues in college can translate into a lifelong battle with eating and health-related issues.

You'll struggle to live in or enjoy the moment and, instead, one thing will always be setting you up for the next. One opportunity will be seen as a stairstep to the next. And the same will be true for your experiences, positions, and even relationships. You could spend your life constantly trying to outdo yourself and/or everyone around you.

Likewise, you'll constantly crave control—and struggle whenever you don't have it. For you, control will be closely associated with power and influence. But what you'll struggle to see is how positional control or authority has a limited reach because *real* power and influence is not manufactured, but earned through relationships, hard work, consistency, and grace.

In the end, your life's work and contribution could amount to having done things that don't make much of a difference in the world. While you may succeed at climbing some social or corporate ladders, you will have failed to make any real difference with your life. And this, of course, plays right into the Enemy's hand.

In fact, he's a lot more likely to help you be successful in your pursuit of status, such that it keeps you completely sidelined and uninvolved in things that might make a difference in a hurting world. If you're distracted, then you're one less person for him to have to be concerned with.

There's just no comparison

The god of status requires that you prove your status by validating yourself through endless striving for greater image, accomplishment, achievement, and honor. And no matter how much of this you improve or amass, it will never be enough.

People crave status because they lack a sense of worth.

The One True God gives you a worth beyond the comparison of status.

He calls you *son*.

He calls you *daughter*.

He calls you *beloved*.

Remember the baptism of His Son?

Jesus had yet to perform any miracles, or call any disciples, or preach any sermons. He had merely lived in relative obscurity for thirty years.

In the world's eyes, He had no status.

He stepped into the water, and as He was baptized, the voice of His Father spoke over Him these words: *"This is my Son, whom I love; with him I am well pleased"* (Matt. 3:17).

This is the gift of an identity of worth, which needs no further status.

He gets the "well done" before the job even starts.

The good news: This same God speaks these same words over your life. But receiving them will require you to abandon your insecurities which constantly say you must work harder to be worthy, more important, more influential, and more powerful than everyone else.

Remember, after His baptism Jesus was immediately led by the Spirit into the wilderness, where He met up with the god of status face-to-face.

god of status: *If you are the son of God . . . prove it. Validate yourself. Show me your power.*

Jesus: *It is written: "Man shall not live on bread alone, but on every word that comes from the mouth of God"* (Matt. 4:4). (Remember the word that came from the mouth of God at His baptism. Jesus had been "eating" those words. We, too, must learn to "eat" those words.)

god of status: *If you are the Son of God* (Matt. 4:6) . . . *Show me your influence* (in other words, get God to prove it.)

Jesus: *It is also written: "Do not put the Lord your God to the test"* (Matt. 4:7).

god of status (looking out over all the kingdoms of the world and their splendor): *"All this I will give you if you will bow down and worship me"* (Matt. 4:9). *Let me control you and I will let you control the world.*

Jesus: *Away from me, [god of status] Satan! For it is written: "Worship the Lord your God, and serve him only"'* (Matt. 4:10).

You see, the One True God is so generous He actually gives us a status no amount of power, influence, or control could ever attain.

It is wrapped up in these baptismal words, *"You are my son. You are my daughter. You are one of my beloved ones. And with you, I am very pleased"* (Matt. 3:17 paraphrased).

This is the heart of God for you.

Believe it. It's worth it.

God's desire to redeem and restore you in this area

I believe God has plans for you. *"Plans to prosper you and not to harm you,"* as we read in the book of Jeremiah. I fully believe that God wants you to be a person of purpose and influence, and that He wants your life to count.

But the truth is that image, power, and influence (status) might very well look different from what you think. And that's where you'll need to be willing to give up your current definition of "success," which is really what you're pursuing when you chase after image and status—because that's a worldly definition of the word.

Throughout the gospels we see Jesus talking about the first becoming last, and the last first. We see Him esteem the slave and bring down the master. What He's describing is a paradigm, a way of thinking, that is upside down by the world's standard. It's a way of living that is contrary to the social economy of our time (just as it was in His time on earth). It's a way of life that looks foolish to the world, but brings honor and glory to God.

And this is the kind of life—and status—that God desires for you.

I believe that God wants you to trust Him with your status in life, and all that entails. I believe He wants you to be comfortable in your own skin and content in the place He currently has you. I believe He wants you to be successful in the place, and in the relationships, that you currently find yourself.

I believe that He wants you to be your very best self—and know that is good enough. That *you* are good enough.

And as you learn to be faithful and content in the places and positions where God has put you, I believe God will use you in new and amazing ways that you would never have dreamed for yourself. In fact, I think we often limit the ways God wants to work in us and through us, because we've allowed our definition of success to be narrowly construed by the world and by the god of status.

Responding to God's invitation

Let's return to Anna's story.

She returned to campus as a new woman, after her liberating spring break experience.

Anna was still involved with a lot of the social circles, activities, and scenes that she had been in before the break, but she seemed to have a new peace about her, a new confidence that was tied to her true identity. She also made significant time for her new relationships, as well as her faith.

Anna went back home for her summer break and found acceptance and affirmation in her liberated reality.

She returned for her senior year with a markedly more noticeable posture towards her faith, her relationships, and the things she chose to give her time to.

It was clear that she was living confidently out of her identity as a child of God and loving life, no longer a servant to the god of status.

Are you ready to relinquish control of your life, and your status, to God?

Are you ready to quit chasing the god of status and trust that as you are proven faithful with the things that God brings into your life? That He will bless and grow you (and your status) in His economy, in ways that bless you and bring honor and glory to Him?

If so, consider how you might take the following steps to help you yield this area of your life to God:

* Confess your obsession with status (image, power, control, etc.) to God. Ask Him to remove this love from your life.
* Ask God to reveal to you any area of your life that you need to address, as it pertains to the pursuit of status.
* Ask God to give you a new heart and a new mind filled with His love and understanding regarding the illusions of status and power.
* Ask God to reveal to you a purpose for your life and the ability to have influence, when and however it is appropriate.
* Ask God to help you reconcile and restore any relationships that may have been damaged as a result of your pursuit of status. Ask your friends to hold you accountable in this area of your life.
* Ask God to give you an awareness of the god of status and how it might try to weasel its way back into a controlling seat in your life. Be willing to talk with a mentor about the challenges this might hold.

God has a way of using the individuals that make themselves available to Him and elevating them to positions of importance and influence in the places He wants to use them. It's not a pursuit that any of us should take up without the timing and leading of God, because with it comes greater levels of responsibility. So as we avail ourselves to God, let us do so in this area with eyes wide open.

THE gOD OF SUBSTANCES

They worshiped their idols, which became a snare to them.

Psalm 106:36

"I have the right to do anything," you say—
but not everything is beneficial. "I have the right to do anything"
—but not everything is constructive.

1 Corinthians 10:23

I had met Lee at some point early in his freshman year, but we didn't really connect until the end of his freshman year, when he was applying to be one of our student leaders for the following academic year.

Over the course of Lee's sophomore year we grew pretty tight, and it was clear then that Lee had a deep and passionate faith in Christ, was excited about learning and leading, and was quite conservative when it came to what he thought ministry leaders should—and should not—be about.

In that regard, he was like many of the leaders I've seen over the course of my years on campus. He was quite convinced of his positions and consistent in living out what he proclaimed to believe.

By the end of his sophomore year, he was ready to re-up his leadership position for the following year. And when he returned for the fall term of his junior year, Lee seemed like the same guy who left campus at the end of his sophomore year, and even more committed to his faith and new leadership position.

But not long into the fall term, Lee began to talk with increasing regularity about his twenty-first birthday that he would be celebrating not long after the first of the new year.

I didn't think much about it at first, but before long it seemed as though Lee was setting out to have quite the birthday bash. He seemed to believe that he had somehow earned the chance to go crazy for a night, since he would be "legal" and all.

This did not go over so well with some of the other student leaders (or staff, for that matter).

The growing concern within our team did serve to open the door for some good conversations about drinking and the personal and public life of the leader, but that also led to further tension and ultimately some division within our team.

Lee's birthday came and went without much conversation, at least around our ministry.

That spring, Lee became increasingly withdrawn and detached from the ministry work and community he had previously been so excited about. The further into the semester we went, the less we saw of Lee.

Lee didn't re-up to lead during his senior year, nor did he come around anymore. Many of the returning leaders who had once been close to Lee claimed that he quit hanging out with them and had taken up with a new crowd.

In their words, *he just wasn't the same Lee anymore.*

>>

Another hallmark of the college experience is experimentation.

After spending most of the first eighteen years of life "becoming someone," students often arrive on campus and begin to evaluate who they are and, subsequently, who they want to become.

Students will experiment with new interests, relationships, hobbies, foods, music, and the like. As they're exposed to new people, places, and opportunities, they will undoubtedly be introduced to new things. Some they will like. Some they will not. And sometimes they will choose to experiment even more.

In many ways, it's a rite of passage. You've moved out from under the protective wing of your parents and a way of life you have always known, and now you're being exposed to much that is new. You have decisions to make as you step out into your new world, and not all of them will be easy. In fact, there will be many opportunities to experiment with things that can be harmful, if not habit-forming, and even illegal.

What I see on campus

Increasingly, I see students walking away from the convictions and values that they had when they arrived on campus, and throwing themselves into what has come to be known as "the college experience" or "college life."

From social drinking to a hardcore party scene, to experimenting with illegal drugs, to other habit-forming substances, too many students seem to leave behind at home their good judgment and ability to discern what is good from what is not.

Some will take longer to get there, but the percentage of students is high, who are approaching their formative college years as years to experiment with substances that are considered "risky."

And it's taking a toll.

Under the guise of "everyone's doing it," students are getting involved with things that are harmful physically, emotionally, mentally, spiritually, and even socially. They believe that by choosing to be a part of the mainstream campus culture, they are paving the way for a great college experience.

Instead, what I see is a generation of students who are bearing the wounds of their decisions to experiment with harmful chemicals, addictive behaviors, and confusing activities. Where many of the campus gods that we have (and will) talk about in this book are not bad in and of themselves, this category might be the exception.

Now, before you write me off as some sort of old, ultra-conservative, out-of-touch pastor dad, let's check the facts:

* The legal drinking age in North America is twenty-one. This makes it illegal for approximately two-thirds of the student body to drink alcohol. Traditional students won't turn twenty-one until sometime during their junior year. So it's not even a matter of "Should I?" until that point.

* Tobacco use, while not illegal, has been proven to be a major contributor to certain kinds of cancers and respiratory diseases. It's is a highly addictive substance that often creates

lifelong users because the nicotine within it is a chemical too difficult for most to give up.
* Drugs are illegal. It's just that simple. And prescription drug abuse (or misuse) is also illegal. That includes sharing and selling your own prescription drugs of every kind. Using on campus will likely lead to severe consequences, which may include suspension or expulsion. It will also likely get you arrested. Then, of course, there are the ways that it messes with your brain and body; most of those ways are forever damaging (and only momentarily enhancing).

And if this is a god that you have been following, you have likely already formed a list of justifications for why your use of one or more of these substances is OK.

I only drink socially.
I only smoke occasionally.
I only use drugs recreationally.
I know my limit and never exceed it.
I can quit anytime I want.
I'm in control.
Jesus drank wine.

Am I right? Are we tracking?

Does any of this sound like you? Maybe someone you know?

What I don't want to do here is give you a list of "do's" and "don'ts," because too many people have relegated faith (and following Jesus) to that very thing.

Instead, let me ask you a few questions:

* If you use one or more of these substances, why? Honestly! Do you have a good, legitimate reason for why you do? What do you get out of it? What is it you hope to achieve in using

> Some **Quick Facts** Related to College Students and Alcohol:
>
> - Each year, 1,825 college students between the ages of 18 and 24 die from alcohol-related unintentional injuries, including motor vehicle crashes.
> - 97,000 students between the ages of 18 and 24 are victims of alcohol-related sexual assault or date rape.
> - 400,000 students between the ages of 18 and 24 had unprotected sex and more than 100,000 students between the ages of 18 and 24 report having been too intoxicated to know if they consented to having sex.
> - About 25% of college students report academic consequences of their drinking, including missing class, falling behind, doing poorly on exams or papers, and receiving lower grades overall.
> - 31% of college students met criteria for a diagnosis of alcohol abuse and 6% for a diagnosis of alcohol dependence in the past 12 months, according to questionnaire-based self-reports about their drinking.
>
> All stats from: www.collegedrinkingprevention.gov, http://tinyurl.com/mzn5ks (accessed 5/24/13).

this substance (to unwind, forget your problems, fit in, loosen up)? Why do *you* use?

* Do you want to become dependent on substances in order to achieve a certain feeling or experience? Don't laugh. It's a serious question. Can you see how that might happen if you consistently use?
* What are you willing to forfeit in life should you become addicted? Seriously. Take a moment to think this through.

Because the reality is that if you live a life where these addictive substances become a constant, you'll be sacrificing a number of other things.

No one—*no one*—starts using substances like this with the thought that it will one day rule their life. *No one plans for that.*

Instead, what most often happens is that people start as recreational users, and before long their body begins to tell them that they need it more often and won't be able to function properly without it.

How it's impacting you now

Like all of the other campus gods, the god of substances is one where the impact will be more noticeable to others than to the one in its clutches.

If you're the one using and abusing substances, the Enemy will lie to you and allow you to believe that it's not an issue.

That you have everything under control.

That no one notices what you're doing.

But to concerned (and even casual) onlookers, especially those closest to you, your changes will be obvious and will, therefore, impact your community.

Given the fact that the substances we're talking about are harmful, habit-forming, and in some cases illegal, there will be certain communities that you will naturally gravitate toward. Why? Because we like to be with people who look, sound, and act like us. We don't often choose to be in regular contact with people who don't participate in what we like, or consistently question our choices, or express disdain for our actions, or challenge our priorities.

Who we connect with—and relate to—often shapes how we will spend our time. If you're someone who consistently uses substances, you will find yourself not just hanging out with people who do that, but getting involved in experiences and going to places that will promote and further reinforce your substance use.

Likewise, choosing to use these kinds of substances will have an impact on other areas of your life: your classwork, job performance, other responsibilities. Depending on which substance(s) you get entangled with, the impact felt in these different areas can be quick and significant.

Am I right? Do you see this happening on your campus or in your own life?

Whether it's a preoccupation with getting your next fix, or needing to sleep off what remains in your system from the night before, or the damage that the substance(s) is having on your brain, if you're entrenched in this lifestyle, you're likely struggling to keep up with classwork and other responsibilities—let alone excel in whatever you are doing.

What starts out as "casual" experimentation can quickly become a full-blown addiction that takes your college experience into a dark and lonely place—a place you never had imagined or intended it would go. And one of the lies you might find yourself believing is that this current lifestyle is a "college thing," and once you graduate you'll calm down, straighten out, and live a more intentional kind of life.

But the truth of the matter is this: the patterns and habits you form during your college years will dictate—yes, *dictate*—the way you live for quite some time after you graduate.

The long-term damage of following the god of substances

What might have started off as a way to fit in or live into the college experience can become the kind of lifelong addiction that ruins relationships, inhibits career success, causes devastating and painful illness, and even leads to premature death.

No one considers that they could get mouth, tongue, throat, and/or lung cancer, or emphysema as a result of their tobacco habits. Nor do they consider what their secondhand smoke might do to those around them.

No one thinks that they could become an alcoholic, develop liver disease, damage their bodily organs, or die of alcohol poisoning or an alcohol-related accident or cancer. Nor do they think that their drinking could have a negative impact on others.

No one believes that they could become a drug addict, which could lead to squandering everything they have in order to get their next fix, losing their job and possessions, losing their family, taking to a life of crime in order to feed their addiction, or possibly even overdosing. Nor do they think about how their drug use could ruin the lives of others around them.

Sure, users of these substances have likely heard the statistics, but none believe that it will ever happen to them. *Or,* they don't care because they're more focused on what the substance can do for them, than what it could potentially do *to* them or to others.

"Social" drinking is becoming more acceptable in a growing number of Christian circles, but here's my word of caution to the college student (Christian or non) claiming to only be a social drinker: more often than not you won't know if or when you're slipping from social drinker status to something more dangerous. If drinking (or smoking, or drug use) is used as a way of coping with life—stress, pressure, depression, sadness, breakups, a bad grade, a tough relationship, a loss, a struggle—then how easy will it be to have "just one more" when things are going especially bad?

And if the use of these substances is associated with celebrating a win; a good grade; a great date; the end of a project, or paper, or term then how easy will it be to turn to that same substance when things aren't going your way, but you want that winning feeling anyway?

Again, you could easily write me off as being a prude in this area. But I hope you won't. I hope you'll give good consideration to why you would use substances to alter yourself, the person that God has made you to be.

If there's a better way of dealing with whatever it is that is driving you or motivating you to use, then I hope you will consider doing that.

And these kinds of choices are much, *much* easier to make during your college years than they are later in life. Because you will likely consider experimenting in college (if not before) in ways that will establish mental links between using and certain feelings, or between using and dealing with certain kinds of situations—such that by the time you are well into your twenties or thirties or beyond, you will not know how to deal with certain situations or achieve certain feelings in any other manner.

Your brain and body will become hardwired to turn to these substances when certain situations and scenarios arise. And the god of substances will give you a growing number of reasons to use.

There's just no comparison

The god of substances preys on your insecurities, issues, anxieties, shortcomings, mishaps, struggles, and tough circumstances, and convinces you that the best way to deal with those things is to self-medicate. *If you want to feel differently than you do—or not feel at all, then you believe a little bit of this will help. And if it doesn't, try more.*

But self-medication is both temporary in relief and habit-forming in practice.

The One True God loves us as He has made us, and wants us to learn how to love and accept ourselves for who we are, and how we have been made, as we are shaped and formed more and more to be like Jesus.

Our confidence, security, and self-worth cannot be found in a bottle, pill, or chemical substance, but in Christ alone. We cannot appropriately deal with our struggles, issues, or tough circumstances by getting lost in the mind-numbing, mood-altering god of substances; this can only be done in and through the grace and mercy of Jesus Christ.

Hear within these words God's incredible love for us and His desire to bring healing and wholeness to our lives:

> *My son, pay attention to what I say; turn your ear to my words. Do not let them out of your sight, keep them within your heart; for they are life to those who find them and health to one's whole body.* (Proverbs 4:20–22)

> *Then they cried to the LORD in their trouble, and he saved them from their distress. He sent out his word and healed them; he rescued them from the grave. Let them give thanks to the LORD for his unfailing love and his wonderful deeds for mankind.* (Psalm 107:19–21)

> *LORD my God, I called to you for help, and you healed me.* (Psalm 30:2)

Praise the Lord, my soul, and forget not all his benefits—who forgives all your sins and heals all your diseases, who redeems your life from the pit and crowns you with love and compassion. (Psalm 103:2–4)

He heals the brokenhearted and binds up their wounds. (Psalm 147:3)

Heal me, Lord, and I will be healed; save me and I will be saved, for you are the one I praise. (Jeremiah 17:14)

"He will wipe every tear from their eyes. There will be no more death" or mourning or crying or pain, for the old order of things has passed away. (Revelation 21:4)

May the God of hope fill you with all joy and peace as you trust in him, so that you may overflow with hope by the power of the Holy Spirit. (Romans 15:13)

Whoever fears the Lord has a secure fortress, and for their children it will be a refuge. (Proverbs 14:26)

Humble yourselves before the Lord, and he will lift you up. (James 4:10)

For the Spirit God gave us does not make us timid, but gives us power, love and self-discipline. (2 Timothy 1:7)

Our God heals our pain, restores our brokenness, and grows in us a confidence and self-worth that is deeply rooted in our identity as a child of God.

This is the overwhelming heart of God for us.

God's desire to redeem and restore you in this area

For all of the other gods that we've talked about in this book, we've been able to identify the good in it. We were able to see how a good thing was wrongly elevated to an inappropriate place in the heart and mind of an individual, such that it caused them to see their lives through that one thing.

When God is given His rightful place as Lord, the false god is seen for what it really is and is put back in its proper place.

But with substance use and abuse, I don't know that there is this same opportunity. The only exception might be social drinking, but again, I've described how that can be a slippery slope for many, in times of stress and pressure.

Cheesy as it may sound, I believe God wants to be for us the very same things we turn to substances hoping to find: something to take the edge off; a pick-me-up; a reason to gather; someone to assist with the stress, pain, and challenges of life; a friend.

But He won't force Himself on us; He waits for us to choose Him over and above any other god.

Responding to God's invitation

You'll recall that as Lee started to experiment with alcohol, he began to distance himself from our ministry team and a number of friends he had been close with since early in his freshman year.

Lee graduated without reconnecting, but because of our social media relationship, I've been able to keep up with him through the occasional update I run across in my news feed.

After graduation, Lee went to graduate school, got married, and ended up serving in a church. Not the type to be too revealing online, Lee has never (to my knowledge) posted anything that would lead me to believe that substances are still a big part of his life. But then again, most people don't post about their struggle with addictive chemicals—unless of course they are party people to their very core.

I hope and pray, for Lee's sake, that his experimentation with alcohol was something he got out of his system while he was on campus, but I don't know that for certain.

>>

Can you relate to Lee's story at all?

Are substances controlling you?

If so, are you ready to surrender them to God?

Are you ready to quit wallowing in a mediocre life with the god of substances, and trust that God has better things in store for you? That God can meet you in your place of need and provide for you in ways that substances can only mask for a short time?

If so, consider how you might take the following steps to help you yield this area of your life to God:

* Confess your dependence on substances to God. Ask Him to remove this unhealthy habit from your life and replace it with something much better.
* Ask God to be your strength and resolve, as you seek to overcome any addictions that have taken root in your life. This will likely include getting the assistance of a professional counselor and/or joining an appropriate support and recovery group. Overcoming chemical addictions is not easy, but with God's help and the support of others who are journeying on a similar path, it can happen.

* Ask God to reveal to you the ways the god of substances has deceived you into relying on substances in certain situations and social settings, in order to feel comfortable in your own skin. Ask Him to help you feel more confident in your identity as His child.
* Ask God to show you any relationships that may have been damaged as a result of your use of substances. Ask Him to help you to restore wounded or broken relationships to a healthy place.
* Ask God to make plain the ways that substances can quickly take control of your life, and then ask Him to remove from you any desire to use them. Ask Him to give you a vision for helping others do the same.

THE gOD OF PLEASURE

Do you not know that your bodies are temples of the Holy Spirit, who is in you, whom you have received from God? You are not your own; you were bought at a price. Therefore honor God with your bodies.

1 Corinthians 6:19–20

At first, Shawn and I knew each other casually through connecting around campus and different events.

One day Shawn popped into my office, something he had never done before. He told me that a colleague had encouraged him to come and talk to me, so I stopped what I was doing and offered to go grab coffee with him.

After we got our drinks, Shawn picked a table outside, off and away from the other outdoor seating. Shawn and I talked and took some time to get to know each other a little more in-depth than we previously had.

And eventually it happened, that awkward pause in the conversation that gives either party the chance to wrap things up or dive into something new. In situations like this with students, I'm usually content to sit in the awkwardness of the moment and allow them to make the choice.

I could tell that Shawn had something on his mind, but that he was getting fidgety and fighting to find the right words to express it. After a couple of minutes and a few uncomfortable glances in my general direction, Shawn asked if he could talk to me about something he had been struggling with. I told him I'd be happy to help him in whatever way I could, so he started in.

I'm struggling with porn, he shared, *and it's getting pretty bad.*

I nodded understandingly, and he continued.

I hate it. I don't want to look at it anymore. But one thing always seems to lead to another, and before I know it I'm sitting in front of my computer, jumping from one website to the next.

I want to stop. Can you help me?

Shawn and I spent some time that day talking about his situation, his disdain for what he was doing, and his desire to stop.

We talked about some practical steps he could take regarding his access to online content, as well as some accountability measures he could establish with a couple of his close friends.

We committed to meet again the following week to talk about how things were going.

When we got back together, Shawn was slow to return to the subject of his struggles. So when the time seemed right, I asked about it.

He glanced down for a moment, and then off into the distance. It was clear our little game plan had not worked very well.

As it turned out, Shawn had only made minimal efforts to deal with his struggle, and therefore he was feeling all the more stuck and like a failure.

We talked that day about the power of sexual addictions. I also told Shawn that I was committed to walking with him through his struggle, and seeing him be successful in overcoming it. I also mentioned that it might be worth talking with a professional counselor and/or getting connected to a local recovery group.

He seemed genuinely relieved and appreciative. So we concocted a new plan for the week ahead and set a future date to connect.

Shawn and I would go on to meet almost weekly that term, and sadly, every meeting had the same general feel and tone. Shawn would confess a struggle to stay committed to the plan we had made, an uncontrollable urge to get online and look at different images and videos, and growing levels of guilt, shame, and failure.

He would also talk about his desire to have a girlfriend, and how he wanted to get this under control before that happened. He knew what he was doing was not setting him up to be healthy in a relationship, but he struggled nonetheless.

Weekly I tried to encourage him, pray for him, extend God's grace, and attempt to think through some other possibilities for the forthcoming week.

We talked about professional counseling, but he didn't think it was necessary.

We talked about a local support group for people struggling with different kinds of sexual addictions, but he didn't think it was for him.

We continued to meet all semester long, because I didn't want to give up on Shawn.

But when the semester ended, so did my contact with Shawn.

I know he returned to campus after the break, but he didn't come around and he didn't respond to any of my attempts to reach out to him.

>>

If I had to identify the number-one false god that is ruining the lives of today's college students, it would have to be the god of pleasure: sex, pornography, and hooking up.

Are you there? Do you know what I'm talking about?

If not, you are definitely in the minority and, statistically speaking, your chances of encountering the god of pleasure are high and your chances of making it out unscathed are slim. I wish this weren't the case, but it's true.

Here are just a few of the statistics I've run across in researching this subject:

- 12% of all websites are pornographic (that's more than 24.5 million sites).[1]
- Every second more than $3,000 is being spent on porn and more than 28,000 Internet users are looking at porn.[2]
- 40 million Americans are regular visitors to porn sites:[3]
  – 1 in 3 are women.[4]
  – 70% of men aged 18 to 24 visit porn sites in a typical month.[5]
- 93% of boys and 62% of girls are exposed to Internet porn before the age of eighteen.[6]

* Only 3% of boys and 17% of girls have never seen Internet pornography.[7]
* The average age of first Internet exposure to pornography is 11 years old.[8]
* 67% of young men and 49% of young women agreed that viewing pornography is acceptable.[9]
* 87% of university students polled have virtual sex, mainly using Instant Messenger, webcam, and telephone.[10]
* Studies consistently estimate that 26–27% of freshmen women have sexual intercourse during at least one hookup. (12% of those partners are ex-boyfriends.)[11]
* Studies estimate that 45–50% of males have sexual intercourse while hooking up over the course of a semester.[12]
* Half of men and women who hookup are seeking a traditional romantic relationship.[13]
* A small minority of students has had more than fifty hookups (3.7% M; 3% F) and six sexual partners (3.5% M; 3% F).[14]
* 11% of modern twenty-five-year-olds have not had premarital sex.[15]
* In highly religious groups, up to 20% successfully wait until marriage.[16]
* In the general population, the ratio of women to men who wait until marriage to have sex seems to be about 60/40.[17]
* Conversely, according to one study found in the American Psychological Association's *Journal of Family Psychology*,[18] couples who waited until marriage to have sex had the following advantages:
  − 22% higher relationship stability
  − 20% higher relationship satisfaction

— 15% better sex ("higher sexual quality of the relationship")
— 12% better communication

Yep, the statistics paint a pretty clear picture. The god of pleasure has gained a legion of followers. He's grown the porn industry into a multibillion-dollar industry. He's convinced young men and women that casual sexual encounters are no big deal. He's tapping into our innate nature as relational beings, and twisting our desire to know and be known into something unhealthy and unhelpful.

And if you're somebody who is being deceived and controlled by the god of pleasure, my heart breaks for you.

The momentary pleasure you might be experiencing now—whether virtual or in the flesh—is not worth it.

Remember, we have an Enemy who has come to destroy us and, from what I am seeing on campus, the god of pleasure is wreaking havoc on countless young lives.

What I see on campus

This is one of the biggest issues I see students struggling with on campuses today.

The Internet has made access to pornography increasingly easy. Once upon a time you had to be willing to walk into a store, go to the magazine rack that had magazines covered up (all except for their names), physically reach up and select one of the magazines (in front of anyone who might be around you), walk with your magazine up to the cashier, and lay out your own money to purchase this kind of material.

But you have likely never had to endure something this vulnerable or revealing in order to view porn. Growing up with access to the online world, statistics would suggest that porn may have very well *found you* during time spent online as a youth. Sadly, it could have been one simple click of the mouse that first led you into this harmful and destructive world.

And once that initial introduction to the seductive world of pornography was made, it likely became all too easy to make return visits.

Porn might have also been what made you curious enough to engage in the hookup culture—the opportunity to experiment in the flesh with what you've only experienced virtually.

No matter the reason, the hookup culture is becoming more normative on today's campuses. With no clear definition, the term "hooking up" can refer to anything from kissing, to fondling, to oral sex or sexual intercourse. Participants often appreciate being able to imagine their exploits as something much bigger, or smaller, than they really were under the protective umbrella of such a vague term.

But make no mistake: the hookup culture is not a harmless playground for a younger generation wanting to explore freedoms and feed urges. And for some, the casual or harmless hookup can serve as an entry into a more explicit sexual scene. Be it one-night stands with a wide variety of partners or a committed (albeit premarital) relationship with someone you see a future with, the kind of mental, emotional, and spiritual damage being done is hard to see or feel in the moment, but no less devastating.

Pornography, hooking up, premarital sex are all ways the god of pleasure seeks to gain and maintain control of us, because we can quickly form habits and even addictions.

And addictions are hard to walk away from.

Addictions are formed when behaviors are repeated, and the chemical responses in our bodies rewire our brains to associate certain actions with certain outcomes. Because you've liked the feelings that are gained by viewing pornography, or hooking up, or having sex (not the shame or guilt or feelings of self-loathing that can arise, but the physical arousal, sexual release, and euphoric dopamine unleashed in the brain), this kind of addiction is incredibly difficult to break.

It's all sexual, but *not* relational.

It speaks to a desire for intimacy that we all have: a desire to be known. As beings that were created by a relational God to be relational, we instinctively crave this. But relationships are hard.

So out of a fear of true intimacy, really getting to know someone in ways that form deep relational bonds, it can be all too tempting to opt for something artificial, something fake, something without substance—because it feels safer.

From the safety you find while sitting behind a screen, or messing around with someone you don't really know, you can pick and choose your "mate" for the moment, and you don't have to worry about rejection. You don't have to worry about saying or doing the wrong thing, or what to do on a date, or what the other person is thinking or feeling.

You can simply engage in a moment of fantasy, fooling yourself into believing there's enough there to stir something within you, while degrading the person (virtual or real) to an object.

Fool yourself no longer; there's no relationship there.

And in reality, you're actually making it increasingly difficult to engage a member of the opposite sex in ways that are formative and fun. The longer your addiction to this kind of pleasure continues, the less likely it will be that you will be able to gain what you really desire: *true love and genuine intimacy.*

How it's impacting you now

In the here and now, your engagement with pornography, hooking up, or having casual sex is beginning to cause you to be socially awkward, emotionally and relationally stunted, and increasingly distant from God.

You walk around campus wondering if anyone knows your secret, or what will happen if you ever get caught in the moment. You're quite sure that people can tell just by looking at you that you're engaged in this kind of activity, so you feel tempted to withdraw further from the crowd.

You find it increasingly challenging to have conversations with others because the images you view online, or secretive experiences you've had behind closed doors, have embedded themselves at the forefront of your memory so what's "on your mind" is eliminated from the topics of conversation, yet it is very present.

Your emotions are wrapped up in your pseudo "romances," and between the highs that it provides in the moment and the lows that might follow (when feelings of shame, guilt, and disgust thrust themselves upon you), you find yourself riding a roller coaster of emotions that won't let you off. This makes it hard to be around others for very long, so you aren't.

And worst of all, your unhealthy activity is causing a growing chasm between you and God, or at least that is how it feels. You know that what you're doing isn't right, and that at some level you're objectifying another one of God's children; but because your experiences are becoming addictions, you're compelled to turn your back on God rather than change your behavior.

Of course, distance from God in one area of your life is ultimately distance from God in all areas of your life. As much as you might try to compartmentalize the different areas and activities, the reality is that you cannot ignore God in one area and expect to find Him in the others.

The long-term damage of following the god of pleasure

The long-term damages will differ from one person to the next, but generally speaking, those who are hooking up, engaging in sex before marriage, or addicted to pornography during their formative college years will struggle in their relationships in the future.

The social awkwardness and inability to communicate or relate to other people will only get worse and, therefore, become magnified.

The intimacy you desire, as well as the opportunity to have a life with a significant other—someone you can grow old with—will be jeopardized by your active engagement and habitual gratification found in these pleasure-producing activities.

One of the lies the god of pleasure feeds its subjects is that once a person enters into a marriage relationship, they'll be able to walk away from those pleasure-producing activities they've been so engrossed in. That because they have someone they can be intimate with they'll have no need for these disconnected (albeit "harmless") experiences anymore.

But it's a lie. Those patterns and habits and addictions are incredibly hard to break, and will be carried into the marriage relationship—should the god of pleasure even allow you to make it that far.

Sure, there might be a season when all is well in the new marriage, but once the newness wears off or once trouble sets in, it will be all too easy to fall back into old ways of thinking and living.

And then, undoubtedly, those spouses caught in cheating relationships, adultery, or using pornography will devastate their loved one.

It's quite likely that the relationship will be damaged to the point of breaking, because the trust and intimacy that a marriage relationship is supposed to engender is a gift that has to be cared for and nurtured. Damage to this takes a devastating toll on a marriage. Restoration is always possible, but it can be a long and painful road.

So why not avoid it if at all possible?

There's just no comparison

The One True God is the Creator of pleasure. It's true!

The same God that created the universe—and all that is within it—designed us to feel, love, desire, and connect. He created us such that we long to be loved and deeply connected to Him and to others.

This same God also designed sex and sexual acts to be both immensely enjoyable and intensely bonding. He designed sexual pleasure and intimate relationships to go together, which is why we read over and over in the Song of Solomon the cautionary word: *do not arouse or awaken love until it so desires.*

The Song of Solomon reads like a steamy romance novel in which two young newlyweds express their bountiful love and affection for one another. The feelings they feel are intense, and can barely be contained, which is why they are compelled to remind the friends who are also a part of this story about the need to not rush into love and all that it includes.

The god of pleasure knows that we have been created as relational beings and that the One True God has designed us to enjoy, and deeply bond through, intimate acts and relationships.

The god of pleasure also knows how easy it is to get hurt within these kinds of deeply personal relationships, so he conspires and attempts to convince us that we should get what we desire physically in ways that keep us safely guarded from the potential emotional pain that can come when we allow ourselves to be vulnerable and intimately known by another.

The god of pleasure tries to convince us that we can separate the gift of pleasure from intimate connection. But we can't. It's a lie.

And truth be told, we shouldn't want to separate pleasure from relationship. This is how God made us. This is what He desires for us: to experience the heights and joys of sexual pleasure and satisfaction within the context of a loving, intimate, God-centered marriage relationship.

But the god of pleasure knows that if he can convince you to try his way—just once—that it will be incredibly difficult to escape his clutches. Because while he promises a no-strings-attached, pleasure-filled experience, he doesn't tend to mention the overwhelming feelings of guilt, shame, and self-loathing that can follow such disconnected acts.

And yet, the One True God makes room for those of us who have fallen prey to the god of pleasure, but want a second chance at approaching intimacy and pleasure God's way.

Consider the story of the woman caught in adultery:

> *. . . Jesus went to the Mount of Olives.*
>
> *At dawn he appeared again in the temple courts, where all the people gathered around him, and he sat down to teach them. The teachers of the law and the Pharisees brought in a woman caught in adultery. They made her stand before the group and said to Jesus, "Teacher, this woman was caught in the act of adultery. In the Law Moses commanded us to stone such women. Now what do*

you say?" They were using this question as a trap, in order to have a basis for accusing him.

But Jesus bent down and started to write on the ground with his finger. When they kept on questioning him, he straightened up and said to them, "Let any one of you who is without sin be the first to throw a stone at her." Again he stooped down and wrote on the ground.

At this, those who heard began to go away one at a time, the older ones first, until only Jesus was left, with the woman still standing there. Jesus straightened up and asked her, "Woman, where are they? Has no one condemned you?"

"No one, sir," she said.

"Then neither do I condemn you," Jesus declared. "Go now and leave your life of sin." (John 8:1–11)

The god of pleasure would tell her that she is dirty, broken, "damaged goods"—but not God.

The One True God knows that no one is perfect and all have sinned, but that to love and live the right way we need to be willing to leave ungodly ways behind and, instead, do things God's way.

God's desire to redeem and restore you in this area

I think this is one of the things that breaks God's heart the most, which is why He wants us to let Him restore us in this area.

God created us as relational beings. He created sex and our sex drive. He made us so that we'd feel strong attraction to others. He designed our bodies to give and receive pleasure. *But God also desires all of these things to be experienced in good and healthy ways.*

Yet in a culture of instant gratification, we struggle to know how to wait, or why to wait, or to believe that waiting is worthwhile.

To believe that we can trust God with our sexual desires and sexual urges is a big deal. But God wants us to trust Him with these very things. God wants to know that we trust Him, that we believe He has a plan for our life, that we believe He can be our portion and our provision, regardless of whether or not we ever get married.

The truth is we can't do anything about the past.

The past is the past. But it doesn't have to define us in the present or dictate our future. God wants to redeem it and restore us.

I believe that God wants to raise up a new generation of young people who are willing to put off their sexual gratification in order to honor Him, in order to love Him, and in order to prepare themselves for healthy relationships and a possible future mate.

No, I don't believe it will be easy, but I believe it's what God wants and, therefore, is worth it.

Responding to God's invitation

Let's revisit Shawn's story.

I regret to share that I am unable to speak to specific details about how Shawn is currently doing, because I simply don't know.

When he pulled back from our relationship and quit responding to my attempts to connect, I was left to wait on him to initiate our reconnection. The reality is that we cannot help people who don't want to be helped.

All false gods know that if they can keep us isolated from truth and community, that they'll likely keep us under their control.

And sadly, not every story has a happy ending—at least not before the student leaves campus.

I don't know that Shawn ever found the help he needed to deal with his pornography addiction. I have heard through the grapevine that he has had a few "serious" relationships since he graduated, but nothing that's ever lasted.

I can't help but wonder if the god of pleasure has something to do with that.

>>

Can you relate to Shawn? Do you find yourself in any part of his story?

Are you ready to yield control of this area of your life to God?

Are you willing to trust that He has something better for your life?

Are you willing to release your past and live into a new future?

If so, here are some steps you might consider as you seek God's redeeming work in your life:

* Call out to God. Let Him know that you're ready for a life change.
* Ask Him to begin healing your heart and mind from the ways the god of pleasure has distorted them.
* Find somebody to talk to. Peers are great accountability partners, but beyond that let me challenge you to find a mentor. If you don't have someone who is older, someone who is wiser, someone who has journeyed through a bit more of life—*find someone.* They are a gift and can offer you prayer and encouragement in this area. They can offer you wisdom as you seek to place God where God belongs in your life.
* Ask God to reveal to you the role that pornography has been playing in your life and how it's been shaping your view of the opposite sex. Ask Him to give you a better vision for success in your relationships.

* Ask Him to help you see the hookup culture for what it really is. Ask Him to reveal to you what it is that you were really looking for in those hollow moments of intimacy.
* If you are engaging in sex outside of marriage, ask God to help you bring that to an end. Ask Him to help you see sex as the gift from God that it is, and how it is meant for the marriage relationship.

THE gOD OF INTIMACY

Guard your heart above all else, for it determines the course of your life.
Proverbs 4:23 NLT

Riley and I met her freshman year, under some of the most painful of circumstances.

She showed up at my office door with her parents. It was her first time back on campus since she had left for fall break two and a half weeks earlier.

Riley had gone home to see her family, friends, and more important, the guy she had been dating for more than three years.

It had been a tough decision for Riley to leave him back home and come to campus, so the first semester was really more of a trial experience to see how being apart would be.

What I found out in talking with Riley's parents, and then heard from her, was that as she was traveling home for her break, her longtime boyfriend was killed in a car accident. She didn't find out until a couple of hours later when she arrived home and, as you might imagine, it completely devastated her.

When we first talked in my office that day, she really didn't have much to say. She struggled to stave off tears, making the comment that she felt she couldn't possibly have anything left in her tear ducts to cry.

Her heart was broken.

She sat there—a lump in a chair—struggling to know why life was still worth living.

Riley and I met daily for the rest of her fall semester, and almost daily for most of her spring semester as well. There was a lot of quiet we endured together. I think she appreciated being with someone who wasn't trying to solve her problem, or make her smile, or suggest to her that she needed to move on.

We took things slow. We talked as she was willing and able.

And much of what she said (when she said it) had to do with life no longer making sense without her late boyfriend.

She couldn't see a way forward. And if there was one, she wasn't sure she wanted to travel it alone.

>>

Do you know the god of intimacy?

This god is a close associate of the god of pleasure we talked about in the previous chapter.

And not long ago these two gods were content to divide and conquer: the god of intimacy primarily focused on women, while

> **Some Quick Facts** Relating to College Students and Relationships:
>
> - 25–40% of all romantic relationships among college students are in some way long-distance.*
> - 29% of singles who fell in love with someone they did not initially find attractive, fell in love after after they had become best friends.*
> - The most common time for breakups is around three to five months.*
> - The number-one cause of breakups on college campuses is cheating.*
> - 32% of college students report dating violence by a previous partner and 21% report violence by a current partner.*
> - 70% of female and 73% of male college students report that they'd like to have a committed relationship.**
>
> * Source: http://tinyurl.com/my5gfwd (accessed 5/29/13).
> ** Source: http://tinyurl.com/ldsrlvr (accessed 5/29/13).

the god of pleasure had its way with the men. But in more recent years—your lifetime, really—these gods have seen fit to knock down the gender walls they had been content to roam within, and pursue any and all potential followers.

Where the god of pleasure tends to focus on the sexual gratification that can be obtained through the physical or virtual connection with another, the god of intimacy tends to exploit our innate design as relational beings and our need to connect with others at an emotional level. More specifically, the god of intimacy sets out to convince us that unless we are with another in ways that create a deep and meaningful connection, then we are somehow incomplete.

Intimacy, in and of itself, is a very good thing. It is a gift of God that allows us to know and be known by another. It allows us to better understand the relational character of God as He relates to His creation, as well as the relational dynamic between God as Father, Son, and Holy Spirit.

Intimacy is one of the gifts that make us, as human beings, unique within God's creation. This capacity allows us to feel bonds with another that are beyond the merely physical. It can include the physical, but registers more in the areas of emotional, mental, and social capacities and needs.

We all have a desire to be known by another intimately. But when that desire becomes the motivating force in our life such that we pursue it and prioritize it above all else, then it becomes something it was never meant to be.

The god of intimacy is a powerful force on college campuses and universities around the world. And as you search for meaning and purpose, the god of intimacy will attempt to convince you that the only place you will find the validation and fulfillment you seek is in the arms of another.

If you buy into this lie, you'll spend your college experience pursuing relationships and cultivating intimacy for all the wrong reasons. It will be self-serving. It won't be about participating in a growing and healthy relationship as much as it will be about not being alone.

God has created us for relationships but His desire is for us to be healthy in our relationships. And He desires to be the Lord of relationships.

When we allow intimacy to become a god in our life, our understanding and expectations of it will become drastically distorted and make much of life difficult.

What I see on campus

I see a lot of insecure young people desperate for the company and companionship of a significant other. This insecurity often drives you to compromise on things you desire, believe, or feel in order to achieve your objective of having someone.

The transition to college is the same for the vast majority of students: new people, in a new place, with a lot of unknowns making life extremely challenging as you attempt to get settled.

And in the midst of transition and instability, the god of intimacy can begin to whisper to you about how things would be much better if you had someone. *God's fine, but He's not going to fill that empty seat next to you in the cafeteria, sit with you late into the night working on homework, or keep you company over the long weekend, so you'd better find a real human being.*

The god of intimacy will go on to suggest that while friends are fine, finding someone special is of greater importance, almost as if it validates you—to yourself and to others.

So you move quickly.

The campus culture and college experience is designed such that it almost facilitates the rapid establishment of relationships, therefore increasing the rate at which intimacy can happen.

This is the first time in life when you can spend as much time as you want with someone. Meals, classes, downtime between classes, evenings, late nights, even overnights. The tables are set such that you could spend most of every day with another person and quickly become attached, if not dependent.

But more often than not, it would seem that most students fail to see where these quick connections might lead. They're not taking the time to get to know their new mate in incremental and measured ways. They're not allowing things to progress slowly over time, and instead they force things to happen quickly and unnaturally.

How it's impacting you now

You may be hard-pressed to see how all if this is really such a big deal.

But it is, indeed, a big deal.

Why? For one, you'll struggle to be alone. Without someone by your side you lack confidence or feel incomplete in some way, almost as if you were without pants. Your insecurity can lend itself to other kinds of mental and emotional anxieties, making it all the more challenging for you to be out in public (or even at home) by yourself.

Learning how to be content when we are not with others is critical. In fact, it is often when we are alone—in silence and solitude—that God works on us in ways that make us better for being in the company of others. It's also when we're alone that God tends to have more of our undivided attention, which betters the chances of us keeping things (like relationships) in their proper place.

Likewise, when you're serving the god of intimacy, your perception of self-worth will be inevitably tied to another. Unless you are with someone, you'll be tempted to believe that you're nothing. And it's not hard to see how this line of thinking could lead you to believe that there's really no "right" person for you, but that anyone will do, really.

In fact, the lie you'll learn to live by is that the right person is the person who is willing to be *with you*—regardless of the reason. You'll be less concerned with growing a healthy relationship and more concerned with keeping your mate with you because you fear the alternative.

So you'll forgo some of your own needs and desires, doing whatever you can to make your significant other confident in your relationship, convinced it's what will bring you joy, contentment, and peace.

But you couldn't be more wrong. And your sense of self and self-worth will be riding a never-ending roller coaster on the status of your current relationship.

The long-term damage of following the god of intimacy

It's probably not too difficult to imagine where this kind of misdirected love and attention can land you, without specific and intentional steps taken to dethrone the god of intimacy.

For one, your ability to function without someone at your side will continue to decline until you quite literally become paralyzed without someone there for you. This kind of relational deterioration, quite obviously, will make you increasingly fearful, controlling, and even neurotic in your relationships. You will become increasingly desperate in your relationships, which will make you an unlikely candidate for anyone looking for something healthy and long-term.

You'll also get to a point where you'll make most (if not all) of your decisions based on the approval of the person you're with, over and above God. Out of necessity, you'll wall God off from your life because you can't risk Him coming into conflict with the other person you're trying to please.

Yep, you'll become the kind of people-pleaser that quite literally will check every decision, both big and small, with the person you're in relationship with. And with God's plans often being so different from our own, the god of intimacy will score a major victory in rendering you (and your life) inconsequential.

All of this will serve to give the god of intimacy more and more control in your life, which will in turn reinforce your fear of being alone. It really becomes a repetitive cycle, maddening in its own right, that will keep you desperate and dependent for intimate relationships, while making you increasingly unappealing to be with.

There's just no comparison

The god of intimacy would like to convince us that we are lacking and incomplete when we don't have a significant other in our life. And if we do have a significant someone, the god of intimacy will attempt to convince us that our security, confidence, and sense of self is wholly tied to that individual and, therefore, that relationship should be given whatever it needs in order to function and flourish, even if that requires sacrificing or subjecting one's self to inhibitive, unhealthy, or even unsafe relational conditions and dynamics.

But the One True God is not like that.

The One True God loves us unconditionally, without reservation or qualification, which is meant to provide us with an appropriate sense of self, confidence, and security that cannot possibly be found in another human being.

Listen to how the Bible talks about God and His love for us, His beloved sons and daughters:

> *Know therefore that the* Lord *your God is God; he is the faithful God, keeping his covenant of love to a thousand generations of those who love him and keep his commandments.* (Deuteronomy 7:9)

I love those who love me, and those who seek me find me. (Proverbs 8:17)

"For I know the plans I have for you," declares the LORD, *"plans to prosper you and not to harm you, plans to give you hope and a future.* (Jeremiah 29:11)

For God so loved the world that he gave his one and only Son, that whoever believes in him shall not perish but have eternal life. (John 3:16)

But God demonstrates his own love for us in this: While we were still sinners, Christ died for us. (Romans 5:8)

But because of his great love for us, God, who is rich in mercy, made us alive with Christ even when we were dead in transgressions—it is by grace you have been saved. (Ephesians 2:4–5)

This is how God showed his love among us: He sent his one and only Son into the world that we might live through him. This is love: not that we loved God, but that he loved us and sent his Son as an atoning sacrifice for our sins. Dear friends, since God so loved us, we also ought to love one another. (1 John 4:9–11)

Give thanks to the God of heaven. His love endures forever. (Psalm 136:26)

So then, just as you received Christ Jesus as Lord, continue to live your lives in him, rooted and built up in him, strengthened in the faith as you were taught, and overflowing with thankfulness. (Colossians 2:6–7)

A new command I give you: Love one another. As I have loved you, so you must love one another. By this everyone will know that you are my disciples, if you love one another. (John 13:34–35)

> *Humble yourselves, therefore, under God's mighty hand, that he may lift you up in due time. Cast all your anxiety on him because he cares for you.* (1 Peter 5:6–7)

This is God's heart for us.

He loves us, wants the very best for us, and simply asks that we choose Him.

He has offered His one and only Son—a perfect Son—for you and for me. He initiated a way for us to get back into right standing with Him because He loves us so much.

God's desire to redeem and restore you in this area

God has always wanted the very best for you, and that includes intimate connections with others. But these connections need to be understood in and through the loving grace of God. It's the only way to see them and experience them for what they really are—a gift.

When we allow God to be the center of our lives, then we're better able to be a healthy contributor to the relationships that God brings into our lives. Where the god of intimacy would suggest that relationships are about what we can get out of them, the God of the universe knows that relationships work best when both parties are looking out for the betterment of the other—while both keep their eyes fixed on Jesus.

But given this definition, it's clear when you look around at the majority of relationships in the world that there are very few that fit this definition of *healthy*. And I think this speaks to how deeply the god of intimacy has managed to embed itself in the hearts and minds of God's people (all people, really).

It is God and God alone who can meet the needs and desires of our heart. Yes, He will likely use other people to fulfill some of those needs and desires, but that's His prerogative and should be left up to Him to decide.

Responding to God's invitation

Knowing all of this doesn't amount to much of anything if we fail to respond to God. He desires to be the Lord of our life, and that means saying no to the lesser gods (like intimacy).

Let's revisit Riley's story, because there's an important detail that I didn't mention, as well as some progress to report.

When Riley's longtime boyfriend was killed in a car accident, she didn't know God. In fact, she was a self-proclaimed atheist.

But somehow, in the midst of all of the pain and chaos, Riley was able to detect God in her presence. And although she didn't know what it all meant, she knew she wanted to be open to God in all of her pain and suffering.

As Riley grieved the loss of someone she had cared for so deeply, she was met by a compassionate and loving God who knew the depths of her despair, and met her there.

There was no instant fix. As I mentioned, we met regularly that year, and spent a lot of time in pain-filled silence.

But we always invited God into our time, and prayed in the time between our meetings, that God would be what Riley needed Him to be: Her portion. Her comforter. Her healer. Her constant companion.

I've stayed in touch with Riley since that time, and am happy to say that God has done (and is doing) a great work in her. He continues to heal her in areas that felt broken and shows her why life is worth living.

That doesn't mean that Riley doesn't still deal with painful memories from time to time. But it does mean that she's able to better see the love and power of God that is so much bigger than any earthly relationship we could ever have.

God used this very painful tragedy to help Riley understand the gift (and not god) that relationships and intimacy are meant to be.

>>

If you've fallen prey to the god of intimacy, call out to God for help.

- Confess where you have looked to relationships (and the intimacy they can provide) when you should have turned to God.
- Ask Him to help you realign your heart to Him above all else.
- Ask Him to give you a healthy perspective on relationships, and keep it.
- Ask Him to guide you in repairing and restoring those relationships that are broken and being used or abused in unhealthy ways.
- Ask Him to help you identify those relationships that need to be dissolved because it's the best way forward for both people.
- Ask God to give you contentment in being alone, because you are known by Him, and that is more than enough.
- Ask God to prepare you to be in relationships and to understand the power and responsibility of intimacy.

God desires for us to experience intimacy—with Him and with others—but it works best when it comes on God's terms and in His timing.

Are you willing to wait on God and surrender this area of your life to Him?

THE gOD OF INFORMATION

What good is it, my brothers and sisters, if someone claims to have faith but has no deeds? Can such faith save them? Suppose a brother or a sister is without clothes and daily food. If one of you says to them, "Go in peace; keep warm and well fed," but does nothing about their physical needs, what good is it? In the same way, faith by itself, if it is not accompanied by action, is dead.

James 2:14–17

Brian and I met early on in his first year on campus. He was a transfer student, and he knew what he wanted and wanted to be about.

Brian and I spent a good bit of time getting to know each other and exploring ways in which he could put his gifts and passions into active leadership around campus.

As that year began to draw towards its inevitable end, Brian informed me that he would be spending the summer in Africa. He had heard some stories from a pair of visiting missionaries at his church and felt like that was where God wanted him to spend his summer.

And although his parents were struggling with the idea of seeing their oldest child go off to such an unfamiliar (not to mention far-off) place, I thought it would be great for him.

Before long Brian was off to serve for the summer in Africa.

And when classes started back up the following fall, I was more than a little surprised to not hear from Brian.

Nothing. Not a word.

A couple of weeks went by, and I happened to be walking across campus, when all of a sudden there he was. He looked a little out of sorts. I told him how happy I was to see him and that I wanted to hear all about his summer. He told me there was a lot to talk about and promised to stop by my office.

Well, a couple more weeks went by before I saw Brian again. And when we did finally connect, Brian seemed almost desperate.

He began to share about his summer in Africa, and how it had changed him. He confessed that he didn't want to return to the States (or school, for that matter) and really only came back because his mom demanded he do so.

He wanted to stay in Africa. In fact, he had been spending most of his time since he had been back in the States—and on campus—trying to figure out how he could get back there as soon as possible.

"Africa needs me!" he insisted.

Brian knew a little about Africa before he left for his summer there, but clearly his eyes had been opened to an unfiltered, non-Americanized story of plight and struggle during his summer of service. So upon his return to the United States, he began to read everything he could access on Africa that lined up with what he had seen and experienced.

He was appalled by what was being reported back in America—and what was not. And he was telling anyone and everyone who would listen.

Brian was convinced that he needed to be in Africa *now*. He didn't want to be at school, and couldn't see how completing his degree could do anyone any good, specially the kids he left behind in Africa. Brian felt implicated by what he had experienced, and so overwhelmed by everything he was uncovering and discovering about the realities of Africa, that all he could envision was getting back to Africa as fast as he possibly could.

>>

It wasn't long ago that students went off to college because they needed information. They went to be exposed to new ideas, and needed to be trained and equipped by professionals and experts to become savvy to the world's ways and ready to make a difference in the working world.

But that's not the case anymore.

With all of the advances in technology, students have access to far more information than they could ever know what to do with. Young people don't need professors, professionals, or experts in order to access ideas, educational content, or instructional know-how.

> Some **Quick Stats** on Our Data Consumption as Americans:
>
> - American households collectively consumed 3.6 zettabytes of information in 2008.
> - The average American consumes thirty-four gigabytes of content and one hundred thousand words of information in a single day.
>   - This doesn't mean we read 100,000 words a day, it means that 100,000 words cross our eyes and ears in a single twenty-four-hour period. That information comes through various channels, including the television, radio, the Web, text messages, and video games.
> - Most Americans consume 11.8 hours of information a day. Overall, from 1980 to 2008, the number of bytes we consume has increased 6% each year, adding up to a 350% increase over twenty-eight years.
>
> Source: A 2009 study from the University of California, San Diego, as reported in the *New York Times*, http://tinyurl.com/yam8dcw (Last accessed 6/4/13).

They simply need an Internet connection and/or access to the right TV stations. And with that, young people can access anything and everything that can be reported on or searched for.

But here's the catch, while they have access to near limitless content, they often struggle to know how to interpret it.

The media like to put their own slant on most of the stories they share and in many instances make choices about what they will and will not cover.

The Internet (for the most part) doesn't filter what is put online. And if you've never been told before, let me be the first to let you in on a little secret: you can't trust everything you read on the Internet.

So, although you no longer need professors, professionals, experts, or mentors to access new ideas and significant material, you do need their assistance in interpreting what it means, what can be trusted, and what exactly you are to do with it all.

What I see on campus

With regard to what most students think they know, I see a lot of arrogance. I know that might seem harsh, but it's true.

I see a lot of students who arrive on campus and don't seem to understand their need for the kind of learning that can happen within the university context. They only see their time on campus as a necessary means to an end.

Is this you? Do you know what I mean?

The god of information looks to sell you the lie that you don't need "these people" for what you want to do. You already know more than they do and if you don't know something, you know how to use Google and YouTube, so why are you paying them all this money?

So instead of going into your classes, organizations, or other interactions with faculty and staff with a moderate level of humility and teachability, you go in with a disgruntled disposition, believing that you're wasting your time and that you won't learn anything new or helpful anyway.

If you're like many students, you know a little about a lot of stuff. You've gleaned some things from articles, blogs, videos, news reports, your friends, and the like, but you've really only scratched the surface of learning and understanding—but you likely don't realize this.

I also see a lot of students who are overwhelmed by what they have been exposed to. Whether you realize it or not, you are almost constantly consuming information, ideas, images, and atrocities at a rate similar to drinking from a fire hose. A small portion of it is landing where it can be processed and understood well, while the majority of it blasts you, washes over you, or completely misses you.

The truth is, you don't know what to do with most of the things you've been exposed to. You don't know how to understand them.

Yet you feel implicated in some way, but aren't exactly sure what to do with those feelings. And here is where I see great potential.

The college years are a sweet spot for recognizing our passions and gifts, and how God might want to use them to meet needs in a hurting world.

But not too surprisingly, that potential can quickly be squelched by feelings of being overwhelmed, under-informed (though that possibility might escape you), and underprepared to do anything about what you have become concerned with.

How it's impacting you now

College and university campuses are one of the richest resources available to you.

Not because they are the keepers and providers of information (as they once were), but because there you will find people whose sole purpose is to help you understand the information you take in, learn how to discern the good information from the bad, and ultimately help you know what to possibly do with it.

But a growing percentage of students are not taking advantage of these resources.

They are failing to see themselves as a work in progress and so they don't pursue, or open themselves up to, opportunities for growth and learning from others (outside of what they might create for themselves). Or they might struggle to see how the assistance of someone older, wiser, and more educated could be of benefit to them. So they go it alone.

And all of this plays right into the hands of the god of information. He wants you to believe that you know enough to do what you want to do in the world. That you're smarter than most of the people around you, and that you don't need, nor can you benefit from, the assistance of others.

He wants you to be a Lone Ranger. And if you get stuck, he wants you to have no one—nor any viable resource—to turn to.

Now, don't misunderstand what I'm saying here. I'm not discounting your intelligence or ability to figure things out. Nor am I suggesting that you hand over control of your life and learning to someone else.

But what I am trying to convey is that you are a work in progress (we all are), and that there is plenty you have to learn from others. So it will be significant for you to consider whom you might invite into your life to help you learn how to filter, think about, discern, and act in accordance with the information you consume. The college campus is rich with these kinds of people.

In many students, I also see an over-confidence in what they think they can accomplish on their own. It's not that they cannot accomplish anything, or that some of them won't accomplish big, *big* things during their college years.

But what I see too much of is students who feel compelled to do something "big" to address an issue they've been awakened to, and who suddenly believe that they have all the answers—and if given the chance, will bring the kind of radical, sweeping change that can produce results overnight.

I don't mean to sound disparaging, but when students jump into the deep end of campus or world issues and propose to bring dramatic change quickly, they often find themselves dismayed by their lack of impact.

Instead of being content with measured involvement and incremental change—and learning more about the depth and complexity of the issue along the way—they bail out when they (or their ideas) are not heard or taken seriously. They become disheartened by their experience and believe change to be impossible.

That's hard to watch.

That's not to say that you can't bring about major change as a college student, but you need to have an awareness of the fact that things might not happen as quickly or as sweepingly as you hope or plan, and therefore it's of great importance to have a Plan B and Plan C in mind.

Again, this is where a mentor-type of individual in your life can help to offer perspective, support, encouragement, and prayer along the way.

In some instances, I see students who shut down because they feel overwhelmed by what they have been exposed to, and don't know what to do with it all.

They skip the activist phase previously mentioned, and jump right into a state of paralysis and hopelessness. They can't (or won't) turn off the information spigot and, instead, continue to allow themselves to be bombarded with information and circumstances that they don't know what to do with. And before they can even attempt some form of restorative action, they are thwarted by the size and scope of what they know . . . and don't know . . . and know that they don't know.

The long—term damage of following the god of information

Years of allowing yourself to be blitzed by the god of information, especially without learning how to filter it, understand it, and utilize it, can lead to a cynical mind. Especially if the information you consume, or even gorge yourself on, is of negative, gross, or evil things.

There is so much that fills the Internet and other news media that is not helpful. There is so much that is damaging, especially if consumed without restriction or reservation.

The temptation can be to chalk up the world—and everything in it, including the God who created it—as a loss. Instead of finding a way to meaningfully engage the world, one could feel compelled to withdraw. You won't see much purpose in anything (including relationships and work) and people (and organizations) will struggle to want you around.

As your mind grows more and more cynical, your heart will grow cold and hard. You will struggle to care about or be impacted by the things that you read and see.

Atrocities, abuses, and terror will not evoke their natural feelings of pain, loss, strife, anger, sadness, or urgency, and will instead be just another bit of information that runs across your eyeballs.

It flashes in, and is gone within an instant. It doesn't register as wrong: it barely registers at all.

And a cynical mind combined with a hardening heart will lead to, at best, a "slacktivist" approach to life.

What do I mean by this?

Simply that you'll feel moved and/or motivated just enough to say something (typically via social media) that registers your feelings about the matter in a public forum. But you won't care enough to do much beyond that and, in many instances, will believe that you've actually done something by voicing your opinion on Facebook or Twitter.

You won't commit anything more than a status update to the matter. You can't. Your cynical mind won't allow you to believe that change is possible and your hardening heart won't allow you to get emotionally involved.

And when this happens, the god of information wins because we have become disengaged from what's happening in the world.

There's just no comparison

The god of information is deceptive, and preys on our desire to be informed and aware of what's going on in the world as well as (in many cases) our desire to be a part of a solution.

This god convinces us that the more we know about *everything*, the better we can help.

But the truth is, as Christ-followers, there are few things that we're all called to do. Consider Jesus' interaction with two sisters:

> *As Jesus and his disciples were on their way, he came to a village where a woman named Martha opened her home to him. She had a sister called Mary, who sat at the Lord's feet listening to what he said. But Martha was distracted by all the preparations that had to be made. She came to him and asked, "Lord, don't you care that my sister has left me to do the work by myself? Tell her to help me!"*

"Martha, Martha," the Lord answered, "you are worried and upset about many things, but few things are needed—or indeed only one. Mary has chosen what is better, and it will not be taken away from her." (Luke 10:38–42)

Note that Jesus is not discounting hard work, or Martha's clear gift of hospitality, but instead is insisting that at *this* moment in time (while Jesus is there with them) Mary had chosen the best use of her time. She had prioritized rightly. She had chosen to sit at the feet of Jesus to be instructed, taught, fed, and encouraged.

This will always be our number-one priority in life (for everyone who calls themselves Christian) because it's what brings right shape, context, and understanding to everything else.

Given the ways in which we were uniquely made with God's specific interweaving of gifts, talents, and passions within us, we are able to better learn how God wants to use us to make a difference in the world.

The apostle Paul shares about this in his first letter to the Christians in Corinth:

There are different kinds of gifts, but the same Spirit distributes them. There are different kinds of service, but the same Lord. There are different kinds of working, but in all of them and in everyone it is the same God at work. (1 Corinthians 12:4–6)

Paul goes on to further illustrate his point by exploring the various parts of the human body, explaining how each one is unique in its role, significant in its own right, and vital to the overall health and function of the body as a whole.

Our God does not expect us to be all things to all people; that's His role.

He does not expect us to save the world; that's His role.

His desire for us is to play our role in His great story. Remember that nothing that is taking place today is outside of His knowledge and ultimate control. He is bigger than any situation or circumstance that we might read about or encounter in this world.

And there will be some things that He wants us to give our time, attention, and efforts to—and many, many others that He will *not* call us to. He wants to use us in specific ways, in specific times and places, to help bring about His Kingdom here on earth.

We are invited to play a supporting role in His grand work. And when we think about it this way, life in a complex world tends to feel a lot less overwhelming.

God's desire to redeem and restore you in this area

God wants more for you.

God wants us to remember that He is God, and we are not. We don't have to be consumed with saving the world because that's His job. That doesn't mean that God doesn't want to use us (and the things we are learning) to meet needs in the world.

But we need to maintain an engaged mind and empathetic heart, which will necessitate that we become guardians of what we allow ourselves to consume. God wants you to be a good steward of what you take in, as well as the resources you have access to right now. You are in a season of life where the ways that you think, believe, and live are being formed and shaped, and will serve to influence your life for many years to come.

So what you take in needs to be understood through a lens of faith. No matter what bit of information you encounter, it's not news to God. And God wants to help you understand it and know how best to respond.

But God can't use us if we've allowed our minds to become cynical and our hearts to grow cold.

Responding to God's invitation

Getting back to Brian's story . . . it took some time and some convincing, but I was ultimately able to help Brian see the value in sticking around for the fall semester as we further explored his future. And the fall semester led to the spring semester, which eventually gave way to Brian's final year on campus.

Over the course of a few months, I was able to help Brian see the value in completing his education, and how that might open more doors for him when (or if) he returned to Africa.

We also began to look at his major, and what room there was in his academic schedule to take some classes on Africa and mission work. I was able to connect him with a faculty member who was very familiar with the region he had spent the summer in and could hopefully serve as someone who would continue to educate Brian on the realities of life in Africa.

Finally, we talked about needing to provide some parameters to Brian's information gluttony, especially as it pertained to Africa. As we conversed about his online habits, it became increasingly clear to both of us that he was doing himself more harm than good with his current consumption levels and methods.

Brian determined that he would give Africa (and his growing love for it) over to God. He committed to trust God to take care of it while he finished school. And he also decided the best thing he could do was grow in his relationship with God and better learn God's heart for Africa, while maintaining a healthy awareness of the current events taking place in the land he had fallen in love with—all while finishing up his degree.

Has information become a god in your life?

Do you consume everything that comes your way without limit or reservation?

Are you humble? Teachable?

Do you struggle to trust God with problems in the world?

If you've fallen prey to the god of information, God can help. Here are a few steps I'd encourage you to consider:

* Share your struggles with God. He already knows, but it helps you to be able to make that acknowledgment to Him. Ask Him to help you know how to set healthy boundaries for your news and media consumption, and why it's important.
* Ask Him to give you a teachable spirit and the ability to see yourself as a work in progress. Always!
* Ask Him to help you know how to understand the things that you see and hear, and how it's supposed to affect the way you think and live.
* Ask Him to help you to know when to take action and when to leave the action to someone else.
* Ask God to bring someone into your life that will share your passions, but who is older and can serve as a mentor to you during this formative season of life.

God wants us to be informed and aware of what's going on around us, but He doesn't want us to be overwhelmed, or worse, paralyzed.

Are you willing to yield this area of your life to Him?

THE gOD OF VOICE

Prayerful answers come from God-loyal people;
the wicked are sewers of abuse.

Proverbs 15:28 (THE MESSAGE)

But I tell you that everyone will have to give account on the day of
judgment for every empty word they have spoken.

Matthew 12:36

If I speak with human eloquence and angelic ecstasy but don't love, I'm
nothing but the creaking of a rusty gate.

1 Corinthians 13:1 (THE MESSAGE)

*Do not let any unwholesome talk come out of your mouths,
but only what is helpful for building others up according to their needs,
that it may benefit those who listen.*

Ephesians 4:29

I met Terry near the end of his freshman year.

I was busy recruiting and interviewing potential leaders for the following academic year. Terry stopped by my office on the recommendation of one of the professors who had suggested that his particular set of gifts and passions could be put to good use within our ministry.

I was glad to meet Terry because we were struggling to find male leaders.

Over the course of my interview with Terry, it became clear that he was sharp, passionate about his faith, and held some growing leadership traits that I knew would fit with where we were heading in the coming year.

Terry was a great leader during his sophomore year, and an "easy ask" to come back for another year of leadership and development.

During Terry's junior year, everyone could tell that he was doing more than just leading students, he was also gaining the attention and admiration of many of his fellow leaders. Terry and I had some good conversations about the significance of his position and capacity to influence. I let him know that he should feel honored, and that although he had not asked for such a role, there was a growing level of responsibility he needed to be aware of.

As the end of Terry's junior year neared, we began to talk about a new position in which he could experience some new levels of leadership and responsibility, something more formal than what he had the year before with his fellow leaders. Terry was both excited and humbled by the opportunity, and he graciously accepted.

But when Terry returned in the fall of his senior year, he seemed to have a bit of an edge to him. As he began to spread his leadership wings, getting familiar with his new role within our ministry, I started to notice a change in Terry's tone of voice and overall disposition. It seemed as though Terry's new position was going to his head.

The year ended up being a pretty tough one for Terry, and for all of us who had to interact with him on a regular basis.

He and I had several conversations about how he was exercising his leadership within the team. We also talked about some of the aggressive and dismissive interactions he had with members of the staff. Terry didn't seem to see the big deal, but said he would try to do better in the future.

Whether he knew it or not, Terry was quickly losing his influence because, increasingly, those around him thought he was acting like a jerk.

I had thoughts of cutting Terry loose, but continued to believe in him and all of the good work he had done in the past. I hoped that maybe this was just a phase he was struggling through, and that he'd get through it soon enough.

>>

The college years are a natural time for finding and further developing your voice. By this, I mean a conglomeration of growing and changing opinions and beliefs, passions and sense of purpose, actions intended to bring about change, and the ability to verbally and convincingly communicate about it to others.

It is a season in which you will see and hear a lot of new ideas that will bring into question ideas you had once held to firmly. It will expose you to new opinions, beliefs, and experiences that will cause you to question what has shaped you, as well as what will shape you in the future.

The college years are a time that can often be described as challenging, freeing, confusing, maddening, exhilarating, frustrating, formative, destructive, liberating, oppressive, empowering, stifling, easy, or overwhelming—given the day or even the time of day.

Nonetheless, you will be asked during these years to speak up and lend your voice and support to different things. People will want to know what you think. People will want to challenge your views, positions, and beliefs. Some will challenge your actions—or lack of actions.

Some **Quick Stats** Related to Students and How They Perceive Themselves:

- 70% of students rated themselves as above average in leadership, and only 2% as below average.
- 60% rated themselves as above average in athletics, while only 6% said below.
- When they rated themselves as to how easy they were to get along with, 25% said they were in the top 1%, 60% said they were in the top 10%, and absolutely no one said they were below average in being easy to get along with.

Stats from the College Board that administers the Scholastic Aptitude Test, the SAT exam, which millions of high school students take each year.

Found at http://tinyurl.com/kercxdz (Last accessed 5/31/13).

And if you're not carefully aware, the god of voice could get you to believing that what you've got to say is important, significant even, over and above most everyone else.

What I see on campus

I see a lack of communication.

Sure, there's a lot of talking going on, but it's not communication. In many scenes and scenarios, it's people talking *at* each other, not *with* each other. There is little (if any) interest in hearing what the other side has to say. They only want to get their point across—loud and clear—and then reiterate it over and over with the intention of verbally beating their opponent into mental and ideological submission.

It's about creating converts to their side, whatever that side may be. This can range from spiritual to political to philosophical to social platforms and positions.

I also see a lot of arrogance.

The student that's following the god of voice tends to believe that they are "in the know," and that most other people need to be set straight. That those people need to be told, in very clear terms, where they have gone astray and what the right way of thinking is.

There is little (if any) consideration for another person's point of view or process of discovery and learning. It's quite simply a matter of right and wrong for these individuals, so if you're in the wrong (according to their opinion), they believe that it is their duty—their responsibility—to correct you.

I also see a lack of teachability.

For those within the grip of the god of voice, they see no need to further educate themselves on much of anything. And they especially don't see how anyone else could have anything to teach them. Any kind of learning will be done through self-discovery. There is little to no sense that they could possibly be in the wrong or that there is more for them to know.

How it's impacting you now

You're not able to hear others who don't think and believe like you, and this is shaping your community.

In many ways you'll see the campus community in terms of "us" and "them." You'll stick close to those who think and sound like you do. Anyone entering your social circle will need to commit to certain ways of knowing and understanding the world. And it will be imperative that they hold to the party line—always.

The "them" in this scenario will be seen as naïve, uninformed, and even ignorant. You'll look down on these individuals as if they've been left out on a big secret, and your only interaction with them will be hostile or patronizing in nature. This will obviously make your social circle increasingly small.

I also see you failing to consider how other ideas and options might lead to something bigger and better, both in you and in the world.

Because you believe you've got it all figured out, you'll see no reason to hear ideas, opinions, or stories that might come into conflict with your current paradigm. You'll balk at those purporting such contradictory things and will feel compelled to verbally belittle their unenlightened thought or position.

Consequently, your closed-off nature will serve to narrow your scope and focus during a season of life when you should be widening it.

The college years are some of the most formative of your life, and you're in a context where a host of differing ideas are being shared and explored. And the truth is that there are very few things that need to be definitively defined during this season of your life.

Even if the way you think during your college years doesn't change, you'll at least become familiar with what it is that others think about different things, and why. You have a chance to learn and grow in ways that can serve to make your own beliefs and way of life clearer and more clearly defined.

The long-term damage of following the god of voice

Failing to see the god of voice for the monster it is, the lifelong follower will inevitably grow into a similar type of creature.

You will thrive on conflict and needing to win.

You will see almost every interaction as a chance to prove your moral and/or intellectual superiority. You'll engage with others until they submit in defeat or simply walk away. You will talk and talk until you've spewed out everything you know (or even make up) regarding the topic of debate.

You will become someone who chooses being right over being in relationship.

The god of voice will convince you that people want to be around winners, which this is the primary reason that you'll think people want to be with you. In reality, however, your obsession with being right and being heard will damage your relationships.

People won't want to be around you because it will become increasingly clear that you don't care about them or what they have to say, and only really want an audience for your various (and unceasing) rants.

Finally, your growth and development will be stunted in numerous areas because you are unwilling to consider anything that varies from what you already know or believe to be true or acceptable.

You will be the same person, or a slight variation thereof, from who you were when you started to dig in and hold firm to your positions and ideas during your college years.

Similar to those who get stuck in a particular decade of music, hairstyle, or sense of fashion, you and your voice will become outdated and/or obnoxious to the point of being more of a farce than someone to be listened to and thoughtfully considered.

There's just no comparison

Just like the god of voice, I believe the One True God wants us to believe that our voice matters.

But the One True God wants what we say to matter, to count, for the right reasons. He wants our voice to be worthy of being heard by others because of what we say, and ultimately, *Who* we represent.

Our voice is one more gift that God has given us to steward. That's right. We have a responsibility to thoughtfully and carefully use the voice that we have been given in the circles of influence the Lord has made possible for us to be a part of.

Consider the following verses regarding how the Bible links wisdom and folly to how we use our voice:

> *Sin is not ended by multiplying words, but the prudent hold their tongues.* (Proverbs 10:19)

Even fools are thought wise if they keep silent, and discerning if they hold their tongues. (Proverbs 17:28)

My dear brothers and sisters, take note of this: Everyone should be quick to listen, slow to speak and slow to become angry. (James 1:19)

Fools find no pleasure in understanding but delight in airing their own opinions. (Proverbs 18:2)

The quiet words of the wise are more to be heeded than the shouts of a ruler of fools. (Ecclesiastes 9:17)

Those who guard their mouths and their tongues keep themselves from calamity. (Proverbs 21:23)

Much dreaming and many words are meaningless. Therefore fear God. (Ecclesiastes 5:7)

Do not be quick with your mouth,
  do not be hasty in your heart
  to utter anything before God.
God is in heaven
  and you are on earth,
  so let your words be few. (Ecclesiastes 5:2)

The tongue has the power of life and death, and those who love it will eat its fruit. (Proverbs 18:21)

Avoid godless chatter, because those who indulge in it will become more and more ungodly. (2 Timothy 2:16)

The One True God encourages us to be thoughtful and intentional in how we use our voice so that when we choose to speak, people will listen.

The god of voice, on the other hand, tricks us into believing that if we can talk louder or with greater confidence than everyone else, then we will have the ear of the people. In reality, however, what we'll have is diminishing levels of trust in our words and our motives.

Both God and the god of voice want us to know that our voice matters, but they suggest two very different approaches to how we should use it. And how we use our voice will ultimately lead to two very different places.

If we truly desire to be people that God uses to influence the world (in both large and small ways) then we must learn how to yield this area of our lives to Him.

God's desire to redeem and restore you in this area

I believe that the voice we've been given is a gift from God. And I also believe that God hopes that we will be good stewards of how we use our voice *and* how we respond to the voice of others.

Our North American culture currently waves the banner of tolerance, believing that this is how we respect the thoughts and beliefs of one another. We get along by *not* sharing those thoughts, values, or beliefs that might cause controversy and conflict. But I think this misses the mark. As a Christian, I believe God calls us to hospitality and charity (as they pertain to voice).

We are hospitable in the ways we create space for people who don't think and believe like we do. We make them feel welcome, valued, and equal. We give them the opportunity to speak and to be heard.

We are charitable in the ways we approach those who don't think and believe like we do, in that we maintain a listening ear, teachable spirit, and openness to the fact that we might be incorrect in our understanding, misinformed, or just plain wrong.

And at the same time we are not afraid to share what we believe and why. We do so with grace, humility, and love. And we do so for a wide variety of reasons.

But it's not about winning, needing to be right, or wanting to hear our own voice. It's about sharing what we have experienced to be true, meaningful, and significant *with grace, humility, and love*, and trusting that God will use our words however He desires.

Responding to God's invitation

By the time Terry was graduating, he thought that he had much of life in the palm of his hand. He knew (almost) everything he needed to know—and he was pretty hard to be around.

Well as it would happen, I randomly ran into Terry several years later.

Terry asked if I had time for lunch, so off we went (though with some reservation on my part, as I wondered if Terry was still the same arrogant and overconfident guy I had seen him become).

It didn't take too long into our lunch conversation for me to realize that Terry was *not* the same guy he was when he graduated. There was a more humble, gracious, and even open tone to his voice.

He shared about how challenging graduate school had been and how he learned a lot. He also shared about his first few years of marriage, and how there was so much compromise involved in making it a loving and peaceful life together.

He even talked a little about some of his initial struggles with his current employer, and how he was glad he chose to stick with the job, because once he got out of his own way he realized just how much he had to learn from her.

Terry had really come a long way.

>>

Has the god of voice made a mess of your life?

Do you feel the need to be the loudest voice in the room? The last to get in a word? The winner of every conversation?

Do you believe that God might want to grow you and teach you through the voice of others?

Do you value or devalue the voice of others?

If you've become a victim of the god of voice, God wants to set things right.

- Voice your struggles to God. Let Him know that you've not been a good steward of the voice you've been given, but you'd like the chance to start afresh and anew.
- Ask Him to help you see the value in the voice of others and to give you the ability to create space for those who think and believe differently than you. Ask Him to broaden your social circles to include people with differing ways of seeing and living in the world.
- Ask Him to replace your arrogance and overconfidence with humility and teachability.
- Ask Him to help you make your words few and worthy of being heard.
- Ask God to help you recognize the relationships that have been hurt or hindered by how you have misused your voice, and then ask Him to help you restore them to right standing.

THE gOD OF (IR)RESPONSIBILITY

Whatever you do, work at it with all your heart, as working for the Lord, not for human masters. . . .
Paul, Colossians 3:23

Laziness brings on deep sleep, and the shiftless go hungry.
Proverbs 19:15

Juen and I met during her sophomore year. She was a leader on campus and a literal tornado of energy and enthusiasm.

During one of the annual involvement fairs that were held at the beginning of the school year, I opted to roam around rather than sit behind a table. In so doing, I found myself constantly bumping into Juen at table after table.

At first I thought she was playing a trick on me by simply running a few tables ahead of me in order to make me think I was losing my mind. But after it happened a fourth time, I looked Juen in the eye and asked her what was going on.

To my surprise, Juen informed me that she had a leadership role in each of the four organizations I had seen her at, plus one more!

I half-jokingly asked how she would find the time to tend to all of her roles and responsibilities. Juen gave a little shrug, an almost sheepish smile, and simply said she wasn't sure.

I didn't know Juen very well at that point in time, so I opted not to host an intervention. But I did tell Juen that I would check in on her later in the semester to see how things were going, and that I indeed hoped it would be a good year for her.

Well, we both got into the busyness of the fall semester, and before I knew it we were nearing the final exam season. While on my way to a meeting across campus one day I happened upon Juen sitting on a curb in the middle of campus. There was a frenzy of activity happening all around her, but she seemed oblivious to it all—almost frozen. It looked as though Juen had been crying.

I quickly decided that I needed to stop and see what I could offer Juen, and that if the conversation ran more than a couple of minutes, it would be OK to show up late to my meeting.

Well, I never made it to that meeting.

As I sat to talk with Juen, she began to cry again, sobbing at times.

When it finally seemed appropriate to ask what was wrong, she took a moment to compose herself, and then simply said that she had made quite a mess of things.

Not knowing what she meant, and believing that she could be talking about 1,001 possible situations or scenarios, I asked if she would care to tell me more.

She proceeded to fill me in on the last few months: about how great things had been back at the start of the semester, and how she had planned it all out so this would be her best term yet. But about the time her leadership responsibilities were starting to kick into full gear, the pace of her class requirements also picked up, with different assignments and a first wave of exams demanding a lot of her time and energy.

Juen was determined to rise above her circumstances, so she hunkered down and didn't sleep for about a week, believing if she could just weather that initial storm she would be OK.

And although she was able to meet all of her leadership responsibilities that week, her assignments were turned in late and she pulled C's on all three of her exams. She wasn't very proud of any of it, but felt that there was plenty of time to regroup and finish well.

She had made it through the initial bluster of academic and leadership activities, but from there, things got worse instead of better.

Juen fell ill and wasn't able to do much for the better part of two weeks. In fact, her parents even came to campus and took her home for a few days.

By the time Juen was back on her feet, she was behind in her academics and desperate to get back up to speed in her assorted activities. She threw herself into all of it, but gave priority to her leadership roles, believing that there were people counting on her for upcoming events and daily direction.

Midterms came and went, and Juen's grades reflected her priorities and two-week illness. She was barely passing her classes.

Juen began to panic but decided to hold off on making any major decisions until she had one more round of exams to try and remedy her poor academic standing.

And wouldn't you know, as that next wave of exams hit, so did the preparations for one of the biggest events she had been charged to oversee. Juen told herself she would do whatever it took to get it all done. But in the end, there just weren't enough hours in the day to do it all.

She made it through the week's events, struggling horribly through her exams, pulling off a good (but not great) event, and finding herself on the verge of illness again.

She called home and broke down as her mom answered the phone. Her parents came and took her home for the weekend, where she filled them in on how her semester had unfolded.

By the end of the weekend, Juen's parents had convinced her that she needed to do anything she could to salvage her grades for the term, quite certain that quitting each of her leadership roles was going to be a necessary step.

Juen initially tried to fight this suggestion, but eventually realized that it was the only way for her to focus on passing her classes.

It devastated her to have to leave her positions midyear, feeling like she was letting down everyone connected to the various organizations. In fact, when I happened upon her she had just broken the news to the last of the five organizations that she had been leading. She was still trying to come to terms with it all.

>>

Like most false gods, the god of (ir)responsibility is a god of confusion and consternation. But this false god is unique from the rest we explore in this book, because it operates out of a split personality—often drawing people to one of two extremes.

At one end, the god of irresponsibility encourages students to fully embrace the season of "emerging adulthood" that we explored in our discussion of the god of freedom. In that chapter we talked about how new freedoms come with corresponding responsibilities, which a growing percentage of eighteen- to twenty-somethings are not interested in taking on. They want the freedom, but not the responsibility.

The god of irresponsibility sees this leaning in some, and gives them a subtle nudge of affirmation in that direction. The lie he spews is that you'll have plenty of time to be an adult (and therefore take on adult-type responsibility) later in life, so no need to bother yourself with that now.

At the other end of the spectrum is the god of responsibility, which at first blush seems less like a false god and much more like a good thing. And at the very least it should be seen as a better option than the god of irresponsibility.

But for the student who gets bitten by the god of responsibility, the ramifications of bowing to this idol can be just as detrimental as the god of irresponsibility. And here's why: what starts off as positive steps toward maturity and growth can quickly snowball into something that is larger than life and out of your control. Responsibility in one area (much like control) can make you crave it in other areas. So you'll be tempted to take on more, and more, and more of it.

And before you know it, you can become upside down with things you are responsible for. For many, paralysis is the common result.

The things you've committed to will suffer. *You* will suffer. But not being prone to give up on things, you'll fight valiantly to keep all of the balls in the air—all of the plates spinning—because you want to keep your commitments. You hope and pray that there is enough of you to go around. But before long, things begin to crash down around you.

Without a doubt, this two-headed idol is one that will figure out which end of the responsibility spectrum you are inclined toward, and will then create an alluring and well-paved path for you to unknowingly meander down.

Yes, the truth of the matter is that the formative college years are a great time for you to begin to take on new levels of responsibility, but in measured and intentional ways. However, it can be all too easy for you to free-fall toward one of these two extremes.

What I see on campus

Irresponsible students are often (but not always) males who get sidetracked with computer or TV screens, sleep, or simply being lazy. This isn't sexist; it just shows how the god of irresponsibility has found something within males that makes them (much more so than most of their female counterparts) easy targets.

Male or female, I don't think most students go away to college with the intention of *not* getting involved, and instead, choosing to spend most of their days and nights hidden away in their dorm room playing games, watching TV and movies, or sleeping their college experience away.

Yet year after year, there are numerous young men (and some young women as well) who end up choosing to spend a majority of their time doing this very thing. The god of irresponsibility gets in

> Some **Quick Facts** about Students and (Ir)responsibility:
>
> Two sides to the same generation—Gen Y:
>
> Kids born in the '80s:
> - Teen pregnancy rates dropped.
> - Drug abuse was lower than their parents.
> - Violent crime was at its lowest level in twenty years.
> - Education and civic involvement was at a record high.
> - Students were optimistic about their prospects of changing the world.
>
> Kids born in the '90s and beyond:
> - More likely to be mavericks.
> - Tend to be lethargic rather than active.
> - Self-absorbed rather than engaged.
>
> Source: Millennials Rising study as found in Tim Elmore's *Generation iY: Our Last Chance to Save Their Future* (Poet Gardener Publishing, 2010), p 31.

their ear and assures them that there will be plenty of time to get to all of those other things like classes, finding a job, making friends, getting involved, and having a social life later on. *For now, let's just play one more game, watch one more episode, or sleep for one more hour.*

And so the god of irresponsibility will begin to slowly, yet methodically, infect every area of your life. What you had initially thought to be a harmless interest in gaming, movies, or taking naps can become an isolating waste of time and opportunities. The highlight of your days will become passing new game levels, quoting more and more memorable lines, and counting down the minutes until you can return to your beloved pillow and down comforter.

The god of irresponsibility is all about keeping you preoccupied with time-wasting experiences, such that you'll fail to grow and mature in important ways that the college experience is designed to help facilitate.

All of this will then keep you tied to, and overly dependent upon, those who sent you off to school. Instead of learning how to manage your life—your money, your schedule, and even your relationships—you'll look to your parents to assist you in every way possible.

And the god of irresponsibility will have you believing that this is how life is supposed to be. That your parents actually appreciate the opportunity to continue to take care of you, albeit from a distance. That graduation is the time to grow up and take on responsibility.

But that's not true.

And then there's the other end of this two-headed monster: responsibility (or better put, over-responsibility).

The overly responsible students are often (but not always) female, who love to be involved, have a hard time saying no to great (or even good) opportunities, and they love being depended upon.

They like to be asked to assist or lead, given increasing levels of responsibility, and freed up to succeed. It makes them feel noticed, valued, and appreciated. Those feelings produce in them an even greater desire to find ways to get involved and assist others.

However, this often leads the overly responsible students to overextend themselves, believing that they have a higher capacity than they actually do.

Success in a few areas can create a number of great opportunities which, again, these students will have a hard time saying no to. And the god of responsibility will convince them that they are the master of their schedule, that they can make room for just one more commitment and that they really don't need that much sleep.

Sadly, this regularly leads the overly responsible student to having to bail out of most of the things they've committed to in order to attempt to salvage their grades, which is their primary reason for being on campus.

They hate this (even though it's the right decision) because there's nothing worse for those who have committed to following the god of responsibility than walking away from unfinished business and unfulfilled expectations.

And the wisdom of this decision is often lost amid the high levels of personal disappointment (let alone any disappointment expressed by the leaders, ministries, organizations, teammates, or relationships they have to walk away from), fear, frustration, anxiety, exhaustion, and an overwhelming sense of failure that they feel.

Yes, the god of responsibility doesn't play fair, and knows exactly how to subtly distract you while leading you to an unengaged and ineffective place.

How it's impacting you now

For the irresponsible student, you're failing to grow and develop in ways that the college years naturally lend themselves to. Because you're wrapped up in your own little world, you're missing out on opportunities to learn good time management, how to prioritize responsibilities and activities, how to live on a budget, and even how to make good friendships. You're neglecting and negating opportunities to live into new levels of independence and self-sufficiency in ways that are measured and appropriate for someone in your stage of life. You're unable to see the value of hard work, self-discipline, and delayed gratification, and instead choose to focus on whatever seems fun, easy, or able to meet your most immediate needs.

For the overly responsible student, you're creating for yourself a lot of unnecessary anxiety and stress. You're struggling to see the value and benefits of finding one or two things to really invest your time, talents, and passions in. You're burning a lot of bridges and relational capital, and having to deal with a lot of shame and pain that could have been avoided with a simple "no."

And in both instances, you're creating for yourself a way of living that can become normative in the present, and a hard routine to break from in the future.

The long-term damage of following the god of (ir)responsibility

For those who fail to free themselves of the god of irresponsibility, the future will be a definite struggle.

You'll likely end up moving back home because it's the option that seems easiest.

You'll struggle to get and/or keep a job because you've not spent much time thinking about or preparing for it. All of the time commitments, responsibilities, and pressure to produce will be a major turn-off for you.

You'll find it hard to maintain relationships with your more responsible friends. You'll see them living the kind of life that you want to have now, but because the god of irresponsibility has embedded its ideas so deeply within you, you'll give up on the idea, believing that it would take too much effort to achieve.

And for those struggling indefinitely with the god of responsibility, the outlook can be just as bleak.

You'll likely develop a complex related to your inability to manage all of the things you believe you should be able to handle.

The god of responsibility will continue to tell you to do more and to take on more, but your inability to produce or juggle it all well will leave you in precarious position after precarious position.

Your relationships (both personal and professional) will be unstable, if not regularly changing, because of what the god of responsibility will demand of you. You'll feel the need to obsess over every detail, and scrutinize every decision, and people will grow tired of listening to your rants about how tired, busy, and stressed you are.

You'll find work rather easily, but struggle to keep employment or find ways to move up. Your obsession and anxiety with smaller loads will get you easily passed over for promotions because your employer will think you lack both confidence and capacity to perform.

But this *doesn't* have to be your future.

There's just no comparison

Whereas the god of (ir)responsibility attempts to push us to one of two extremes, knowing that the side of us that prefers life to be clean and clear would rather have all of the control, or none of it, the One True God invites us to be co-laborers with Christ.

It's an incredible invitation when you stop and think about it; the God of the universe is inviting you and me to join with Him in cocreating.

God does not expect for us to make our own way in this world. And at the same time, God has no plan to do everything in this life for us. He wants to work with us, partner with us, to create something special—something extraordinary!

But it requires that we leave the two comfortable ends of the god of (ir)responsibility and enter into this gray area in which we are constantly needing to discern what is *our* work, and what is *God's* work.

And that can be challenging. In part, because it requires that we be so in tune with God's work in our midst that we can decipher what God wants us to do, and what it is that He wants us to let Him do.

In many ways it's like a dance. A dance where God leads and our job is to keep in step. We have a role to play, but it's not the lead role. Our job is to follow in the steps of the Lead.

Hear the Lord's invitation to us all:

Jesus went through all the towns and villages, teaching in their synagogues, proclaiming the good news of the kingdom and healing every disease and sickness. When he saw the crowds, he had compassion on them, because they were harassed and helpless, like sheep without a shepherd. Then he said to his disciples, "The harvest is plentiful but the workers are few. Ask the Lord of the harvest, therefore, to send out workers into his harvest field." (Matthew 9:35–38)

And then be assured that this work He invites us to join Him in will not overwhelm us:

Come to me, all you who are weary and burdened, and I will give you rest. Take my yoke upon you and learn from me, for I am gentle and humble in heart, and you will find rest for your souls. For my yoke is easy and my burden is light. (Matthew 11:28–30)

God's desire to redeem and restore you in this area

I believe that God wants us to be good stewards of our time, energy, and efforts.

But the evidence, and near universal acceptance, of this relatively new season of life known as "emerging adulthood" seems to speak to how deeply the god of (ir)responsibility has embedded itself within the fabric of the North American culture.

Where the god of responsibility was once the dominant force of this two-headed idol, it is clear the god of irresponsibility has now taken over, and the number of students failing to make the most of their formative college years is growing.

Yet all is not lost; God is just as big and just as capable of working in the lives of college students as He has always been.

Our challenge becomes understanding how to work with God to see the deceptive nature of this dualistic god by learning how to step into appropriate levels of responsibility, while still taking times of leisure and Sabbath to enjoy the season of life that you're in.

Truthfully, God wants both for us. He wants us to be responsible. Not for everything. But definitely for some things, and an increasing number of things (for the college student) in ways that are healthy, formative, and appropriate.

He also wants us to enjoy down times. Times when we can goof off, play around, and have fun during this transitional season of life. God wants us to work hard *and* play hard. God wants us to experience the joy and freedom that can be found in the flexible schedule of college life.

And God also wants us to become more familiar with the practice of Sabbath and taking a Sabbath rest.

The biggest challenge is learning to listen for God's leading as you live responsibly, which includes the essential elements of rest and recreation.

Responding to God's invitation

Let's jump back into Juen's story.

When we left off, she was a shell of the overly responsible young lady she had previously been.

Juen went on to finish her fall semester well, passing all of her classes—and spent her spring semester working toward reestablishing her academic standing while only participating in (and not leading) a couple of different activities.

For her junior and senior years, Juen was chosen to be a resident assistant, a very challenging and demanding leadership role on campus. But it was the only thing—outside of classes and her social life—that she committed herself to. And it paid; Juen was a stellar RA!

She also excelled in her coursework during her final two years on campus, even graduating with honors.

Juen learned a lot from that painful semester of overcommitment. Be she also didn't allow it to dictate her future.

God used her pain to produce a young lady who was learning to trust Him with her life and the things she would commit herself to.

>>

Can you relate to Juen's story?

Or maybe it's the god of irresponsibility that's been menacing your life?

If the god of (ir)responsibility has led you to one of these two extremes, know that God can help. God wants you to be healthy and happy, learning how to be appropriately responsible as you grow and develop as a college student.

If you've fallen prey to the god of (ir)responsibility, God wants to help you.

* Ask God to examine your life and help you see where this false god has misguided you toward unhealthy ways of thinking and living.
* Ask Him to help you see the value in responsibility (if that's been your struggle), or rest and recreation (if that's been your struggle). Ask Him to give you a vision for a balanced life as it pertains to these things.
* Ask Him to help you see where your time, energy, and efforts would be best spent, and then invest fully in those places.
* Ask God to help you prioritize your life in ways that honor and glorify Him and benefit you as well.
* Invite your friends to hold you accountable to your new commitments to be either more or less involved.
* Talk with a mentor about how significant their ability to find balance in this area has been. And if they confess that they don't do a very good job living into appropriate levels of responsibility, rest, and recreation, see what you can learn from their struggle and encourage them in this important effort.

Learning how to live a well-balanced life in this way during your formative college years has the potential to set you up well for a healthy, fruitful, and enjoyable life.

THE gOD OF NEW

I have seen all the things that are done under the sun; all of them are meaningless, a chasing after the wind.

Ecclesiastes 1:14

Sophi, like a lot of students I've gotten to know, liked nice things.

She came from a well-to-do family that had afforded her a very comfortable lifestyle growing up. And when she moved off to college, they wanted her to continue to be comfortable, but requested that the credit card they gave her be used only for necessities.

Sophi did a good job of keeping her spending in check during her first semester on campus. But with the start of the spring term and a new set of classes, Sophi suddenly found herself in a new social circle—and feeling the need to spend more money in order to fit in with her new friends.

Sophi had nice things, and she even had new things, but she felt compelled to stay at the front edge of the latest fashion trends. She liked her new friends and wanted to make sure they continued to like her.

And so she spent.

And spent.

And spent.

Before she knew it, Sophi had racked up quite a credit card bill. And since the bill came to her, and not her parents, they didn't know what kind of financial trouble she was getting herself into.

Well, Sophi didn't return to campus that next year. I later learned from one of her friends that things got so bad (financially) for her that she broke down and told her parents everything, shortly after she moved home for the summer break.

As a result, Sophi was required to stay home, find a job, and work until she had fully paid off the debt she had accrued.

>>

I think it's natural to be curious and even excited about new things: relationships, homes, jobs, cars, phones, computers, outfits, books, babies ... you name it.

New things are exciting precisely because they are new.

Materially speaking, we get excited because we've never experienced this thing, or maybe the latest version of this thing. We're excited to explore all of the possibilities it holds and learn how it has changed (and gotten better) by comparison to the last one we had, drove, or lived in. We're excited, in part, because we think it's going to make our lives easier or better—or both.

New relationships bring an opportunity for new adventures, new conversations, new ideas, and new possibilities. We're excited to learn all of the ways in which we are similar, as well as those ways in which we are not. We are excited to see how bonds form and feelings develop as more time is spent together, more stories are explored, and more experiences are shared.

Even new jobs or leadership positions can come with their own exciting potential. New relationships and networking. New growth opportunities and learning. New levels of responsibility and leadership. New possibilities as they relate to the future.

And since we have a God who is constantly making all things new, it makes perfect sense that this would be something we are naturally drawn to. It is a chance for us, in some ways, to better understand God as Creator. It's also a chance for us to better understand ourselves as people created in the image of God.

But like many good things, there is always the potential to elevate the gift to an unhealthy place, over and above the Gift Giver. And in this case we make a god out of "new" and the pursuit of all things new.

What I see on campus

I see students who are preoccupied with the newest and next, with the latest and greatest.

This isn't a new development in the college world, but the combination of multiple media interfaces (and their incessant advertisements), an American culture of entitlement, and an

> **Some Quick Facts for College Students and the Pursuit of New:**
>
> This year college students will spend over $60 billion on their everyday needs, including:
> - $1.99 billion on collegiate-branded items
> - $3.41 billion on shoes
> - $5.31 billion on dorm room furnishings
> - $6.63 billion on clothes and accessories
> - $2.99 billion on electronics and computer-related equipment
> - $5.5 billion on alcohol
> - $326 million on renting DVDs
> - $341 million on video games
> - $474 million on music
> - $600 million On-Demand Movies
> - $658 million on movie theater tickets
>
> Source: eCampus.com infographic found at http://tinyurl.com/n3pgslk (Last accessed 6/7/13).

overwhelming desire to fit in can all lead to an unhealthy expectation of what you can and should have during your college years.

The Internet alone is filled with sites designed to help you browse for your next upgrade. From gadgets to girlfriends, handbags to husbands, books, movies, wardrobes, hairstyles, body products, and more—there are an unending number of ways to spend your time and money in the pursuit of something new.

And it's causing a lot of students to wonder and worry if they are wearing and carrying the right things. If they're being seen with the right people. If there's something more they could be doing to ready themselves for their dream job.

They struggle to be content or even present in the present, and always seem to have their eye on the next prize.

What strikes me most about this is that there seem to be so many students who talk a lot about pushing back against societal norms and pressures. Yet, for some reason, many seem unable to recognize how easily they conform to the cultural flow in a number of areas of life.

And at some point, this duplicitous way of life is going to birth a great tension within—a tension that the god of new will fight hard to win.

How it's impacting you now

As the god of new establishes its reign, you'll begin to notice a number of unhealthy characteristics and consequences popping up.

For starters, it will begin to grow in you a stronger and more persuasive sense of entitlement. You'll see something, and believe you should have it. *Now!*

Without consideration for whether or not you really need it, or what it might cost to attain it, you can become fixated on getting what you don't currently have.

And those things that you do have—relationships, possessions, experiences—quickly begin to pale in comparison to what is looming just beyond your grasp.

This will lead you to become increasingly consumeristic and materialistic in nature. You'll begin to see people, places, and things much like items on a menu: yours for the taking and consuming.

You'll lose the ability to find joy in any of these things, always believing that there's something better for you just around the next corner. This means that you will hold things loosely, even carelessly, believing that everything (and everyone) can be easily replaced.

And even though you're a college student, you'll struggle to believe that delayed gratification is something that you should have to practice. So you'll pursue new things, no matter the cost. This will inevitably lead to damaged relationships, missed opportunities, and a closet full of unfulfilling items.

You'll find yourself in a world of debt, and the god of new will convince you that the next thing (whatever it may be) will be what fulfills the need you have.

The long-term damage of following the god of new

The unbridled reign of the god of new in your life will eventually yield in you a life of always wanting and never feeling content.

Your emotions will be tied to your possessions (of which you would include people), and your ability to obtain the newest and best. Your life will be put on a running loop, shortsighted and insignificant, that will create a very shallow existence.

Your obsession with new will shape where and why you work, as well as how you will steward your money and possessions. You'll pursue jobs, not for the kind of work you can do in the world, but for what it can provide for you: powerful relationships, unfathomable experiences, and a disposable income that will afford you any luxury you desire.

Your life will be all about *you*, and feeding your desire for new. Your life will be filled with toys, shallow relationships, and countless experiences that you cannot recall.

And inside you will feel unfulfilled and empty.

There's just no comparison

The god of new can keep us on a quest for the newest and the next, knowing full well that our appetites will never be satisfied.

But the One True God has come that we might, *"have life, and have it to the full"* (John 10:10).

The God of the universe wants us to have a full life, not a life full of stuff.

I think that's why the book of Ecclesiastes is included in the Bible. It's a rather odd book, if you've never read it before, filled almost entirely with what biblical scholars refer to as "cynical wisdom."

It's twelve chapters that record the account of King Solomon's quest for "new." What does he have to say?

It's all meaningless; a chasing after the wind.

Solomon goes on and on about his pursuits, naming many of the gods we've identified within this book, proclaiming that all of them have amounted to nothing.

Achievement.

Pleasure.

Status.

Information.

Relationships.

They're all in there—and they all amount to nothing.

Again, it's an odd book to be included in the Bible, and one that might leave the casual reader feeling confused about our purpose and pursuits in life, or even the meaning of life at all.

It's not until the final two verses of this book that its cynical nature is revealed and Solomon's true finding is unveiled: that apart from God, *all of life is meaningless*. A chasing after the wind.

Solomon declares:

Now all has been heard; here is the conclusion of the matter: Fear God and keep his commandments, for this is the duty of all mankind. For God will bring every deed into judgment, including every hidden thing, whether it is good or evil.
(Ecclesiastes 12:13–14)

Suddenly the entirety of the book—all that has been described as meaningless and a chasing after the wind—is recast in light of fearing God and following His commandments.

It is only *in* God, and *through* God, that all things—our achievements, our pleasure, our status, our pursuit of knowledge and information, our relationships, *all* things—take shape and have right meaning.

So whether we're pursuing new things, or learning to be content with what we already know and have, it is the One True God who brings all other things into their proper place and position.

No lesser god even comes close to doing this.

God's desire to redeem and restore you in this area

Did you know that God is constantly making things new? It's true. That's what He does.

And the same is true of us.

We are a work in progress. Or maybe I should say, a work in process.

Because the truth is we're not all making positive steps forward.

We're not all progressing, at least as it pertains to being conformed and transformed more and more into the image and likeness of Christ. When we opt to follow a lesser god, this is what happens.

But God wants more for you. So much more!

He wants to restore your understanding of who you are—and Whose you are—as your primary identity. When this happens we're better able to see and understand the things of this world for what they really are.

He wants to help you understand what it means to be holy and set apart, and that this means often living differently than the world around us.

God wants to help you see the beauty in the *now* in your relationships, experiences, and even your possessions. He wants to help you value them appropriately and prioritize them rightly.

He also wants you to grow in your capacity to be content with what you have, and who you have, in your life. This will lead you to a more peaceful way of life. One that doesn't necessitate you chasing after meaning*less* things, or even meaning*ful* things, for the wrong reasons.

God's invitation is to a way of life that puts Him above all else, values people, enjoys experiences, and appreciates all that you are blessed with.

Nothing in this life is a given. It's all a gift!

Responding to God's Invitation

While Sophi didn't return to campus her sophomore year, she did for her junior year.

Not wanting her to lose ground academically, her parents encouraged her to enroll in the local community college while she worked full time to pay down her credit card debt.

Her parents paid for credits at the community college, with the understanding that if she returned to her original institution, she'd be helping to pay her way through her final two years.

Sophi's parents recognized that they may not have made the best choices with their daughter as it related to her ability to manage her money, as well as her expectations regarding what she should afford herself during her college years.

They recognized their misstep in providing Sophi almost everything she requested during her growing-up years, and wished they had talked to her more about their own upbringing and the role delayed gratification played in their young adult life and early marriage.

Sophi learned a number of important lessons during her fifteen-month stint at home. The Sophi who returned to campus her junior year was clearly more financially savvy, but also seemed to be considerably more content with what she had and appreciative of the education she was receiving, as well as the friends she was walking through life with.

>>

Does your life resemble Sophi's in any way?

Has the god of new caused you to struggle in your ability to be content with what you have, what you do, or who you're with?

I believe God's desire is for us to be content in all circumstances, regardless of what they are.

He doesn't want us to find our identity in anything but Him.

This doesn't mean that we cannot pursue new things (relationships, experiences, and possessions), but it does mean that we need to be aware of our motivations in pursuing what we pursue, as well as what the pursuit is doing to us within.

Are you willing to get out from under the control of the god of new and rebuild your life on your identity as a child of God?

If so, here are some steps I'd encourage you to consider:

* Ask God to illuminate the areas of your life that this false god has warped and worn away in you. Ask God to bring healing and wholeness to those areas.
* Ask Him to help you see the value in being content—in every circumstance and situation, and what it means to appreciate with greater value those things (people, experiences, and possessions) that you have been blessed with.
* Ask Him to help you invest your energies and efforts in things that matter.
* Ask God to give you a vision for your life that is far greater than mere consumerism.
* Seek out accountability in this evolving area of your life.
* Ask a mentor to share their experiences with delayed gratification, and also self-denial, as it pertains to the pursuit of new things.

LAST WORDS >>

A NEW CREATION

*"For I know the plans I have for you," declares the L*ORD*,
"plans to prosper you and not to harm you, plans to give you hope
and a future. Then you will call on me and come and pray to me,
and I will listen to you. You will seek me and find me when you seek me
with all your heart. I will be found by you," declares the L*ORD*,
"and will bring you back from captivity."*

Jeremiah 29:11–14

*Do not conform to the pattern of this world, but be transformed
by the renewing of your mind. Then you will be able to test and
approve what God's will is—his good, pleasing and perfect will.*

Romans 12:2

*Therefore, if anyone is in Christ, the new creation has come:
The old has gone, the new is here!*

2 Corinthians 5:17

Becoming a new creation is both an instantaneous event and an ongoing process.

When we come to believe in Jesus as the Son of God and Savior of the world, our life changes in an instant.

We are much like that younger son from the story of the prodigal son that we read about in the chapter on freedom. After demanding his share of the family estate, skipping town, and squandering everything he had on frivolous living, he turned back towards home.

And when his father saw him, still off at a distance, he went running towards him.

I love the way Mumford & Sons captures this in the same song that served to shape the basis for this book. Back in the introduction I mentioned the song "Roll Away Your Stone." Remember me mentioning a vivid and poetic expression of the reality of the human condition? And the song writers using words like darkness, and hole, and soul, and substance, and void, and character as they attempted to describe and understand the world?

They could tell that life involves a search for something, and yet the search is complicated by an overwhelming darkness.

And my intention in writing this book was to expose you to some of the false gods—those dark things that populate the college campus and attempt to fill a hole that only God can fill.

Well, Mumford & Sons go on later in the same song to offer words of hope, while at the same time painting a picture of a God who will not force Himself on us, but patiently waits for us to choose Him.

From the moment we choose God, He is there. And everything is different. New.

And yet, in many ways, it continues on just as it did before.

What I mean by that is that although God is *with* us and *for* us, it doesn't (in most cases, anyway) do away with ways of knowing and living that have become familiar to us.

We can still be tempted by the same false gods—with the same lies and misleadings that we believed and struggled with before—but we no longer fight these battles alone.

We have a loving God who's ready to walk into battle with us.

You are a new creation

This is the beginning, middle, and end of what you need to take away from this book: You are a new creation in Christ Jesus. The old has gone and the new has come.

This means that we need to be reminded to see ourselves as God does.

We need to understand that this identity is meant to shape *everything* for us—much, much more so than the messages of the world or the hollow promises of any false god we might be tempted to follow.

We, therefore, need to ask God to help us see and understand the world as He does. We need to see God's creation as a work in progress, being transformed and renewed in its own right, moment by moment.

And we need to see ourselves as implicated in this process, and as tools that God can use in bringing about His new creation. Yes, even as a college student.

This, then, means that we need to make ourselves available to God, to be used by Him in ways *He* desires. We need to ask God to replace our current priorities with His, to give us a heart that beats for the same things His heart beats for.

And this, of course, means casting off all lesser gods.

Walking in freedom

As we walk in freedom we must be mindful of the fact that God has plans for our lives; plans to prosper us, and not to harm us.

And this is precisely where the false gods fall short, every single time.

They will attempt to convince you that they're looking out for your best interests, but they're not. Their interests lie in seeing you get sidetracked with meaningless pursuits during your formative college years, and thereby derailed from the plans God has for your life.

The false gods know how significant these years are. So a big part of walking in freedom becomes the daily practice of being transformed by the renewing of our minds. Being conscious of what we take in, how we understand it, and how it shapes the way we live.

Now is the time to put a stake in the ground and claim your life for Christ and Christ's purposes. It's time to put all false gods on notice.

NOTES

1. Ed Stetzer, "Pornification: Just the Facts." *Christianity Today*, August 10, 2011. http://www.christianitytoday.com/edstetzer/2011/august/pornification-just-facts.html.
2. Ibid.
3. Ibid.
4. Ibid.
5. Ibid.
6. http://www.covenanteyes.com/lemonade/wp-content/uploads/2010/08/Teens-and-Porn-Infographic.png.
7. Ibid.
8. http://www.xxxchurch.com/teens/stats.html.
9. http://www.covenanteyes.com/2009/11/23/generation-xxx-survey-shows-porn-acceptance-and-use-among-college-students/.
10. "Campus Kiss and Tell" University and College Sex Survey. Released on February 14, 2006. <http://www.campuskiss.com/default.aspx?survey=show&homepage=true>).
11. http://www.hookingupsmart.com/2012/08/06/hookingup realities/the-definitive-survey-of-college-students-sexual-behavior-by-gender/.
12. Ibid.
13. Ibid.
14. Ibid.

15. http://waitingtillmarriage.org/4-cool-statistics-about-abstinence-in-the-usa/.
16. Ibid.
17. Ibid.
18. http://www.theglobeandmail.com/life/the-hot-button/couples-who-wait-report-better-sex-lives/article1847555/.